The New and Selected Yuri

The New and Selected Yuri

Writing From Peeling Till Now

poems and stories
by

Yuri Kageyama

First Printing

Published in the United States of America by Ishmael Reed Publishing Company.

Library of Congress Control Number: 2011902824
ISBN: Hardcover   978-1-4535-4156-2
               Softcover   978-1-4535-4155-5

Please address inquires to:

> Ishmael Reed Publishing Company
> P.O. Box 3288
> Berkeley, California 94703
> U.S.A.
> ireedpub@yahoo.com
>
> Project editor: Carla Blank
> Original photo: Annette Borromeo Dorfman
> Original art: Annette Borromeo Dorfman

This book was printed in the United States of America.

To order additional copies of this book, contact:
Xlibris Corporation
1-888-795-4274
www.Xlibris.com
Orders@Xlibris.com
63199

Table of Contents

For Suzushi Hanayagi, Carla Blank, Isaku Kageyama, Winchester
Nii Tete and all those who aren't afraid to cross boundaries

The Question

Do we write to live or live to write?
Do we write to remember or do we write to forget?
Do we write to remember or do we write to be remembered?
Do we write so we don't kill
or do we write so we don't kill ourselves?
Do we make movies to live or live to make movies?
Do we make music to live or live to make music?
Do we write to live or live to write?
Do we live?
Do we live?
Do we live?

The Yuricane

They've called Yuri "cute" often during her life. She's cute all right. Like a tornado is cute. Like a hurricane is cute. This Yuricane. I found that out when she was a student at the University of California at Berkeley in the 1970s. One of her poems about iconic white women became an underground hit on campus.

In 2009 the audience at New York City's Bowery Poetry Club was also blown away by her poem, "Little YELLOW Slut," a devastating look at the way Asian women are depicted in the media.

The New and Selected Yuri includes poems like this; the manner by which Japanese women are imprisoned behind a "Noh mask," but Kageyama doesn't leave it at that.

Unlike many American Gender First feminists, she is capable of understanding how men are also victims of outmoded customs, though they are not dismissed merely as "reproductive machines," as one minister was caught saying in an unguarded moment. Women should be "quiet" and have bok choy ready when the men come home from drinking with the boys.

It's also the women, who bear the miscarriages, the abortions, the rapes, the beatings from a father, who, years later, can't give an explanation for why he did it. In the United States, the white men who own the media and Hollywood blame the brutality against women on the poor and minority men. White middle class women, and their selected minority women, who want to remain on their payrolls in business, politics and academia, have become surrogates in this effort.

Courageously, Yuri Kageyama debunks this myth and correctly calls out men of all backgrounds and classes as women abusers. The father who inflicts gratuitous punishment upon his daughter is a NASA scientist.

These poems are honest. Blunt. When she says that writing a poem is like taking "a bungee jump," she means it.

Very few of the world poets have Yuri Kageyama's range. Her poems critique Japanese as well as American society. The Chikan. The arrogance of the gaijin, who, even when guests in a country, insist that everybody be like them. Some are erotic. You might find allusions to Richard Wright, Michelangelo, John Coltrane. Music is not only entertainment but like something that one injects, something that invades the nervous system.

I asked writer Haki Madhubuti, what he meant by African Centrism. He said that it was based upon selecting the best of African traditions.

Some of Yuri Kageyama's poems might be considered Nippon Centric. She wants to jettison those customs that oppress both men and women, especially the women, and keep those of value. The Kakijun, The Enryo and The Iki.

Ishmael Reed
Oakland, California
July 8, 2010

Introduction

The first poem I ever got published was "Big White Bitch," in the 1978 edition of Berkeley literary magazine *Y'Bird*, co-edited by Ishmael Reed and Al Young, a piece that's too politically incorrect by today's standards but can be clearly categorized as nonwhite female expression _ probably one of the hardest places to be in embarking on a literary life.

But it is one of those wonders of the literary life that it was a poem I wrote as "a companion piece" of sorts to that poem three decades later, "Little YELLOW Slut," that brought me in touch again with Reed and his partner Carla Blank.

Racial stereotypes and sexuality have always been my obsessions. They are the themes that steer my works and help me explore what is important to me _ how social divisions get defined, how racism and sexism scar people, although we all seek love, understanding and meaning.

Although art is ultimately about transcending the barriers created by human evil, I believe in confronting racist stereotypes and sexist abuses through the personal account.

I also believe artistic statements can be made by juxtaposing subcultures, such as the minority experience in the U.S. and the Japanese life described in the English language, to make for unique works that challenge the mainstream, both in content and in form.

I have always written in the English language because, although I was born in Japan, I grew up partly in the U.S., and my parents always made a point of sending me to international schools when we lived in Japan.

They were relatively ahead of their time in seeing Japan as too sexist to offer lucrative opportunities for women, and wanting to arm me with English fluency to pursue a global career, preferably in engineering or the sciences.

But what I always loved to do was write. The first stories I wrote were in elementary school, when I took the voice of an inanimate or nonhuman object like a pen or a frog, and made up stories about their adventures in the first-person.

I kept writing. I wrote with frenzy. I got published in many literary magazines and anthologies. I did readings and collaborated with visual artists, musicians and dancers in the San Francisco Bay Area in the 1970s and 1980s.

I wrote about the tragedy of the stiflingly narrow definitions of art in community politics. I wrote about sexuality and about music, which sometimes seemed to become one and the same thing in my works.

Reed published some of those poems in a 1988 collection called *Peeling*.

By that time, I had moved to Tokyo to work for a newspaper. I had become a mother, and I was busy. I was so busy I wasn't as determined or sure as I had been that I was a poet.

But I kept writing. I even got some fascinating opportunities to read with poets in Japan like Shuntaro Tanikawa, Shozu Ben and Sachiko Yoshihara, who were very supportive of my work.

I also spent some time working as a journalist in Detroit in the 1990s, during which I wrote mostly about life in Japan and its psychological constraints. My works raise questions about sexuality as defined by one's own eroticism, that is, one's own body and mind, versus the oppressive gender roles, such as those rigidly defined by Japanese society and the sexist status quo.

My story "Seeds of Betrayal," published by Geraldine Kudaka in *On a Bed of Rice* during this period, falls into this category, as does my essay on Tokyo train gropers that Reed published in his 1997 anthology, *MultiAmerica*.

In recent years, my son's growing up and becoming an artist himself, a musician playing with Tokyo-based taiko (traditional drum) group Amanojaku, led by Yoichi Watanabe, helped me rediscover my writing once again _ and with renewed vigor and insight.

After all, a mother must show by example. Or maybe I just wanted to share in the fun. I did want to show my son Isaku Kageyama that there was nothing to be afraid of and that getting up there was what life is all about.

I began reading with younger Japanese musicians at Tokyo clubs, some of them my son's friends. I made a movie of those readings with director Yoshiaki Tago, *Talking TAIKO*, which was completed in 2010.

Talking TAIKO is about my poems. But it also features music by Hybrid Soul, Isaku's rock/taiko group with Chris Young and Pat Glynn, and his collaborations with Winchester Nii Tete, from the Addy-Amo-Boye family of drummers from Ghana, who has nicknamed me "Mom" and is one of the greatest accompanists to my readings I have ever had.

When he was a toddler, Isaku would promise to build a house for me, filled with books, music and lots of flowers. I still try to have literature, good music and flowers, even if they're sometimes just weeds, in our home, which is not a house but an apartment in Tokyo.

By trying to give as a mother, I ended up reaping unexpected benefits. By trying to hand down the legacy of art, I received the gift of art, taking the lead from my son and his talented colleagues.

I had come full circle.

I have also always felt that Reed and I were together in poetic spirit, despite the years and miles apart.

I saw Reed and his family in Japan when he came to read his poems with Kip Hanrahan's band in 2003. I also got together with Reed, Blank and their daughter and poet Tennessee during their earlier visit in the 1990s.

"See? She looks the same," Reed said, smiling with relief.

Reed was writing poems in Japanese. We wandered around Tokyo together with Richie Flores.

Then a few years ago, Blank asked for help in her project of documenting the life and work of Japanese choreographer and dancer Suzushi Hanayagi, with whom Blank collaborated in the 1960s and 1970s.

Blank was gracious enough to ask me to submit a short story to an anthology Reed and she were putting together, *POW-WOW: Charting the Fault Lines in the American Experience—Short Fiction from Then to Now*.

In 2009, Robert Wilson, for whom Hanayagi had worked as choreographer, created, with Blank, an homage for Hanayagi: *KOOL—Dancing in My Mi*nd. Hanayagi now has Alzheimer's and is in an institution.

I went to New York to see the performance at the Guggenheim Museum. I had helped a little with translating Hanayagi's words that expressed her approach to dance.

I was deeply moved by Hanayagi's person and art. I saw footage of her dance both in classical and modern experimental styles, and was awed by her vision to blend the Japanese with the American, as well as the everyday with high art, in an intuitive, natural and honest way.

Reed decided to have a book party for *POW-WOW* at the same time as the *KOOL* performance.

My story in that anthology, which is included in this book, is "The Father and The Son," a chronicle of a woman's thoughts about the death of her abusive father and the confused love affair of her son.

It made me proud, although the stories are merely arranged by alphabetical order of writers' names, that my story comes right after a story by Zora Neale Hurston in that collection.

For the book party at the Bowery Poetry Club, I read "Little YELLOW Slut" with Eric Kamau Gravatt, who flew in from Minneapolis, and Teruyuki and Haruna Kawabata, a Japanese couple on their honeymoon, who were in the U.S. for the first time.

Reed liked the poem and published it in his *Konch*.

I had come full circle _ the same way this book brings it all together.

People don't really change over the years. Never mind that the potential for metamorphosis is eternal. That sounds like a contradiction, but it isn't.

The essence of what I have pursued in my writing remains the same. In childhood or motherhood, what I stand for is the same.

Yuri Kageyama
Tokyo
2011

SuperMom: A Poem for All Working Women With Children

SuperMom is the Mother in "The Terminator,"
  fearless, sinewy, a mother like no other.
SuperMom risks her life to save her child.
SuperMom risks her life to save the world.
SuperMom _ the mother of all mothers.
SuperMom, Mother, Mama, Imamin, Okaasan!
SuperMom is never found in kitchens barefoot
  and wears boots to march to work.
SuperMom doesn't make obento.
SuperMom shops at Ichi-Maru-Kyu.
SuperMom _ the mother of invention.
SuperMom, Mother, Mama, Imamin, Okaasan!
SuperMom doesn't gossip with other moms
  but makes her own money, pays tuition and buys you sneakers.
SuperMom doesn't aspire to be on the cover of "Nikkei Woman."
SuperMom just minds her keep.
SuperMom _ a motherfucking worker.
SuperMom, Mother, Mama, Imamin, Okaasan!
SuperMom endures, her womb red and heavy and big
  and open, wrenching out babies and seaweed and stench.
SuperMom spurts out curdled milk like a fountain in the desert.
SuperMom is the origin of origins.
SuperMom _ the bottom of the sea.
SuperMom, Mother, Mama, Imamin, Okaasan!
SuperMom teaches the primordial instinct of nurturing
  the species, the legacy of creation, the courage of the Artist.
SuperMom shows by example.
SuperMom leaves the message that nothing counts
  except Who You Are.
SuperMom _ the bottom of the earth.
SuperMom, Mother, Mama, Imamin, Okaasan!

My Mother Takes a Bath

My mother
Sits
In the round uterine
   rippling green water
   hazy vapor gray dampness
   soapy smelling
   in the air _ a circle cloud _ above
   the tub of a bath
   the wet old wood
   sending sweet stenches
   sometimes piercing to her nose and sometimes
   swimming in the hot, hot water
   tingling numb at the toes and fingertips
   when she moves too quickly but
   lukewarm caught in the folds of her white white belly
Her face is brown-spotted
   beautiful with dewdrop beads of sweat lined neatly where
   her forehead joins her black wavy tired hair
   and above her brown-pink lips
   one drop lazily hangs, droops over,
   sticking teasingly to her wrinkle
   then pling! falls gently
   playfully disappears into the water
She sighs
And touches her temple
   high and naked
   runs her fingers over the lines deep
Her hand
   has stiff knuckles
   enlarged joints crinkled and hardened
   but her thick nails thaw in the water and
   her hand is
   light

against her face
and gentle and knowing
and the palm
next to her bony thumb
is soft
Her breasts are blue-white clear
    with soft brown nipples that dance
    floating with the movements of the
    waves of the little ocean tub
    slowly, a step behind time, slowly
She sighs again
    thinking of her life,
    was it wasted?
    living for her husband and children?
    no, it wasn't wasted, she thinks,
    I have had a good life
    to have a good husband
    and such good children
This warm spot she has to herself
This warm time she has to think
She cuddles her shoulders like a fetus
    still blind, unborn
Her haunches sway
    rubbing the tub's skin
    soft brown peeling furs of wood
    little jazzed feelers in the water
Her feet are like minimized french rolls, a pair
    coarse and brown on the outside
    warm, good, sweet within
She moves ever so slightly
    to go deeper into the heat
    till her neck is covered
    so
    her chin, an oversized umeboshi, barely shows
Her head sticks out
    noble
Her hands neatly
    politely
    clasped over her knees

jutting awkward awkward from her legs
   the way her elbows do from her arms
Her face from the side
   the cheekbones distinct
   is an Egyptian sculpture profile
   an erotic Utamaro ukiyoe
She sighs
Deeply
And
My mother forgets the passing of time and ages
As she sits alone
With the water singing koto strings in her ears.

For women only

perfume,
rubbing shoulders,
we rattle silently over the tracks
blouses, tucked bags, even powdered chins,
up too close to really see;
we sense only relief
we smell no greasy beards or sweaty suits or
beer breath of the morning after _
this morning commuter train
"josei senyo sha"
reserved
for women only,
introduced to protect the gentler sex
from those groping dark hands
preying prying fingers, stroking thigh,
poking panties,
pretending to be penises
right in public transport,
"josei senyo sha"
this is the kindness of Japanese society:
let chikan go unchecked,
forgiven for their mischief,
and give us, women, this special spot
farthest from the action
farthest from the ticket gates
the first car up front,
and the most dangerous
if we crash

Loving Younger Men

Only the bodies of young men aroused her;
the pure innocence in their wide dark eyes,
the wild still animal strength in their muscles,
the smoothness of their skin, so shiny, stretched
out over their boy-like shoulders, flat stomachs,
abdominals rippling gently, their thick thighs
that could thrust forever into the night, their
soft moist lips, where their tongues, so delicious,
dwelt, which darted against, into her vagina,
making her moan with joy, forgetting everything,
which felt so strong against her own tongue at one
moment, yet another, seemed to melt like caramel
in the back of her throat,
their dry fingers, that touched her in the most
unexpected and expecting spots,
their penises, half-covered by their black curls,
seemed smaller, less developed, less threatening,
yet as their shoulders strangely widened
when they held her, their penises filled her,
pointed against her deepest uterine insides,
hurting her with a pleasurable pain, as though
she could sense with her hand, their movements
from outside her belly. Her father beat her as a girl.
She ran from him, crying, please don't hit me! please
don't hit me! No, rather she stood defiant, silent,
silent tears drunk down her chest, till he, in anger
or fear,
slapped her again and again, once so hard she was
swung across the room, once on her left ear so
that she could not hear for three weeks. She
frequented bars, searching for young men who desired
her. She sat alone drinking. She preferred
the pretty effeminate types _ perfectly featured,

a Michelangelo creation, island faces with coral eyes,
faces of unknown tribal child-princes. To escape
her family, she eloped at sixteen, with an alcoholic.
who tortured her every night, binding her with ropes,
sticking his penis into her mouth until she choked,
hitting her face into bruises, kicking her in
the stomach, aborting her child, his child.
The young boys' heads, she would hold, after orgasm,
rocking them in her arms. She would kiss the side of their
tanned necks, breathe in the ocean scent of their hair,
lick their ear lobes and inside their ears. When they
fell asleep, sprawled like a puppy upon her sheets,
their mouths open, she would lie awake watching,
watching, watching, admiring their bodies, how so
aesthetically formed, balanced, textured. What
she enjoyed the most was their fondling her breasts,
suckling, massaging the flesh, flicking the tongue
against the nipple, biting, sucking till her nipples
were red-hot for days. She could come just by this,
without penetration.
When she is alone, she cries. In the dark, she reaches
upwards, into the air, grabbing nothing.

After the Storm

the man who raped Miu got arrested
he was following women from the convenience store
his face was there on the security camera
she told her story over and over
until the policewoman cried

Teru and Haruna got married
she wore a red kimono and a giant wig
he got sick and shaved after he lost his job
they went to the Grand Canyon for their honeymoon
he has another job now

Mary, executive vice president, has never been married
her mother, who taught her men weren't to be trusted,
died last year of cancer and she met Joe,
a college professor, who holds her hand
they are getting a dog

after the storm
pine needles carpet a silent earth
broken wounds of a ruthless wind
forgetful, still, and all is well
like the ending of a movie

rocket scientist

people sometimes laugh when they learn
my father was a rocket scientist
my father was also a child-beater
this is not a laughing matter
people think abusers are alcoholic degenerates,
unemployed high-school dropouts or drug addicts
who swing their wives around the room
clutching their hair and beating them
and beat the kid while at it
but my father needed to get violent because
he was under stress on his job
he worked for the Apollo program
you know the one when Armstrong the astronaut talks about
the one giant leap for mankind
he was one of the first Japanese who got to work for NASA
that's why I have a bit of a Southern accent
when I say words like: "you all" or "Alabama" or "NASA"
his office was at the Redstone Arsenal in Huntsville, Alabama
everyone in my school worked for the military or for NASA
we still have an autographed photo of von Braun
when we got back to Japan,
he was on TV to talk about our trip to the moon
I wasn't that proud but my mother was proud
I was more scared about saying the wrong thing and
setting him off
it was mysterious—I never figured it out
one moment, he was joking, so witty and sharp
just like a rocket scientist
a jolly roly-poly guy
but he would change
and I would feel a fat whack against my head
it would get so infinitely dark before my eyes
inside my cavernous buzzing head

like I was swimming and spinning into outer space
and I would see tiny sparkling stars
he didn't drink or do drugs
he was a rocket scientist
when I got older and got the nerve
I asked him why he had done that
what was he thinking?
I wanted to know
and he said he didn't know
he helped us get to the moon but
the rocket scientist didn't know
he couldn't remember why he hit me at all

Seeds of Betrayal

Since our move to Japan, you have gotten to digging in the yard, the black, fungus-like earth. It's a neurotic habit. Our neighbors must wonder how many aborted babies, or stolen ones, we have buried. You have planted an avocado sapling, gladiolus bulbs. There is no order to the arrangement as though a schizophrenic has been at work.

A pumpkin vine sprouts. Undoubtedly, a castaway of leftovers from our pungent kitchen sink included seeds gouged out from orange flesh. Under the lazy sun, the tentacles grow, gripping innocent stems, shadowing bushes with its huge drooping leaves.

Our Japanese neighbors clip and water their tiny lawns, plant pansies in neat polite rows on both sides of their gate.

In our garden, the jungle stirs and spreads, all knowing, pulsating a force so bizarre any garden keeper would turn away in shame.

"I can't stand it anymore. I have to tell you," he says, a scrunched boy-look in his flushed face. "I have to tell you because I am scared. They're after me, and I need your help."

It takes a while to sink in.

For the past several months, he has been slipping out at night on his bicycle, roaming the streets, "talking to anything that moved." Most of the women ran away.

One laughed when he offered to give her a ride home. He spoke to her in his broken Japanese, she in her broken English. They walked, hand in hand, in the moonlight, a married man pushing a bicycle, and a woman, who, as it turned out, was also married.

She was flattered. She was flirting, maybe hoping to tell her husband and watch his jealousy.

They paused, and he kissed her hand, then he kissed her mouth.

She had the red painted mouth most Japanese women have, swimming listlessly in her masklike ivory face. She was skinny, waist pinched, frail shoulders caved in, perfect for draping a kimono.

She was like the others. They swore to a conformity that made them predictable and reassuring. If ankle boots were in, they all wore ankle boots. They all dutifully carried Louis Vuitton bags. They kept hemlines high, barely missing their asses, as though God had created them for a lifetime of squeaky clean prostitution.

"All this time, I was into you, too," he says.

"Did you want to have sex with them?" I ask.

"Yes," he replies, probably wishing he hadn't as soon as he said it.

After that encounter, he really couldn't stop. He kept going out, pedaling fiercely, searching for that stranger who'd lust for him at first sight. While he pedaled, the humid wind brushing against his cheeks, he felt free.

Now, he believes she was a setup by the police. The word is out and they're investigating, possibly trying to pin a murder, a rape, or worse, on him.

"I may be stupid, but I'm not a rapist. I don't eat children," he says over and over.

At first, I was surprisingly calm. I had expected the worst after his introduction. He was a serial killer. He wanted a divorce. He wasn't who I thought he was all this time.

We sit in our moldy-smelling kitchen, facing each other across the table.

You didn't break any laws, I assured him. You're just imagining things. Maybe it's just the local right-wing gangsters who're peeved you've harassed their bar girls. If you feel like people are staring, well, Japanese society is small, everyone knows everyone's business. But at this point, it's all hearsay. It's not against the law to ride around in a bicycle, even at three in the morning. And if you approached women and they ran away, well, you could have been asking for directions.

He wants us to move into the bedroom and turn on the radio. He believes the house is bugged. They're listening to our conversation.

"People have been coming into our house. They have our keys. I've set up traps for them so I know. The Kanezaki's, their son has been following me. They have this light shining right toward out door, every night. They're spying on me. I've gone out toward the back, and I know they're listening. They're spreading rumors about me, that I kidnap kids and molest them. You know those signs about beware of 'chikan' _ that was me."

The Japanese have a word for sexual harassers, "chikan," those dirty old men who can't resist their hands on crowded trains, those men who stop their cars and offer a ride.

"Don't heed sweet words on dark streets," the signs on the telephone poles warned.

He got a sense of power out of parading around wearing shorts without underwear, believing that his phallic organ dangled in a daring exhibitionism. All the women he approached, he has lost count. He returned over and over to talk to one with dyed hair in an all-night coffee shop because she didn't act scared and he believed she was a prostitute.

Why? He doesn't know why. Perhaps if he went to a shrink, he or she would explain why. He would like to know.

Perhaps it was because too many Japanese had asked him where he worked. And he didn't have the right answers like Mitsubishi or Toyota. If he was unemployed and just teaching English at home while taking care of the house, he might as well be a criminal, child molester or worse.

Perhaps it just got to be too much, separating the garbage between "burnable" and "non-burnable," putting them out on specific corners on specific days.

Tokyo streets were parodies, right off "Blade Runner," surreal, without angst, without pathos. The salarymen with greasy hair and Armani suits all had breaths that stank of fermented rice. They would totter through train-station platforms, stoop over a bench and puke.

It was easy for him to look down upon Japanese men. But he looked down on Japanese women with a vengeance. They giggled coquettishly, served food they had cooked, waiting wide-eyed for approval. And, because he was gaijin, a foreigner, he thought he could get away with anything. They seemed in awe of him, the casual way he dressed, his defiant mannerisms, his carefree lifestyle, his unconventional marriage.

Of course, he knows now, he was wrong. He believes arrest is imminent. Sweat breaks out on his palms. He hears helicopters. Now, I am beginning to hear them, flapping over our roof. We see dark-suited mustached men following us, swishing by on their cars, almost running us over.

We talk into the night about possibly fabricated evidence, pore over the newspaper crime pages to second-guess what he is being suspected of. We shudder at those famous frame-ups in Japan, like Mr. Menda, whose death-row case turned out to be a mistake.

I can barely keep my eyes open. I can no longer add the simplest numbers. I can barely stand. Nothing is ever what you think it is.

The Kabuki play was directed by and starred Ennosuke Ichikawa III. Like most Kabuki plays, it made no pretense at realism. But it made a great story.

A loving young couple gets separated when the man is tricked into borrowing money and ends up killing the villain in a fit of rage. The man's life is spared, but he is exiled. The man and his beautiful wife send each other long letters on rice-paper scrolls.

Many, many years later, he returns, a hobbling old man. He is to meet his wife at their old home at a certain time. He shows up early. So does she. They both look at the cherry tree they had planted years ago, a mere twig of a tree now heavy with blossoms. They write poems on pieces of paper and hang them from the tree.

The audience laughs because the two keep bowing to each other but don't recognize each other _ until the old man starts rubbing his nose, a habit he had since his youth.

"Oh, it is you," she cries out.

The audience fights back tears.

We are sitting side by side, staring at the painted faces. His hand reaches over my shoulder, tugging it.

"We'll be just like that when we get older," he whispers into my ear.

Was it Shuntaro Tanikawa who observed that married couples have the most perverse sex? It's the comfort of knowing, years of knowing, even the exact words you mumble in your sleep.

You know the precise spots in my body that scream for your reptile tongue, your strong callused fingers, your penis. You knead with knowing hands the pale doughy folds of my stomach that still remember, with fading translucent stretch marks, housing your fetus.

We know what to do. How to exactly time our moves, a ritual numbing in its pleasurable sameness. I know how you prefer your penis licked, where it must lodge in the throat, while I slither my tongue busily, until you moan like a woman. How my nipples must brush against your thighs as I suck until you arch your back or hold my head still to thrust.

In your weathered age, you know how to use the wooden phallic instrument, shaking it wildly in time to frantic agitation, so that by the time your penis enters, my brain has soared, seeping, my nipples are erect, reaching, my legs are spread wide, not caring how those less knowing may be aghast at such whorish joy.

"I just want you to come a lot," you whisper. "I love you. Come, come."

And there's no time, then or later, to ask why you believe this so passionately, or whether this is love or a delusion of trapped dependence, why it seems more a ritual, as though you are my partner, not in life, but in this moment.

He would masturbate, fantasizing about the Japanese women.

One woman he was genuinely attracted to was a religion student. He had coffee with her once.

"But I was real cool," he explained.

She was petite and had chiseled features. More important, she was smarter than the rest.

But now, he thinks she was a setup, too. She had been too aggressive, talking about J.D. Salinger and claiming to be a Jimi Hendrix fan. Obviously, the police had done their homework. But when he'd mention a tune or an album title, he drew only blank stares. Her paper in English on "Catcher in the Rye" made no sense.

For a while, he had gladly answered her phone calls. "Hello, Yumiko," he would say with a cheerful ring in his voice. They all had those names that ended in "ko," which means "child." He was beginning to giggle, like them.

Even after he grew to cowering in the house, worrying about the police, we got letters from the women.

"She is worried about you. Please telephone my friend," one woman wrote in round ink handwriting. "Why do you stop teaching English? I enjoy speaking English."

Our bedtime ritual always crescendos in violence. There is no whip, no dripping candle, no fists, no guns, no calls to the police. One's motive is to hurt, while the other's is to endure. Until the hurting and the enduring can't last. The one intent on hurting is spent. The enduring one is silent, having begged too long for forgiveness.

You remember those times we talked about separation.

You held a hand over your face, muttering, "You're going to suck on some other guy's dick." Yet, other times, you said you enjoyed imagining my sleeping with someone else. You would play voyeur, you said, peeking through the keyhole.

When I imagined a separation, my vagina would get wet. After you had ejaculated, I would beg you to use your fingers so that I would know that you were always there.

I lie awake, my body blending into the cold sheets, floating weightless. The darkness stretches, a liquid universe where gnarled octopi and swaying anemones dwell.

I squeeze my legs, letting my vagina tighten against nothing, stirring like an ember into the warm spot inside of me, a numbness trickling up my crotch until it fills my womb with blood and joy. My hairs stretch, slithering through follicles, creatures with their own lives planted by an unknown hand.

I pull on my breasts, pinching my nipples, and imagine a love that never fails.

Little YELLOW Slut

You know her:
That Little YELLOW Slut, proudly gleefully
YELLOW-ly hanging on Big Master's arm,
War bride, geisha,
GI's home away from home,
Whore for last samurai,
Hula dancer with seaweed hair,
Yoko Ohno,
Akihabara cafe maid,
Hi-Hi Puffy Ami/Yumi,
Kawaiiii like keitai,
Back-up dancer for Gwen Stefani,
Your real-life Second Life avatar
Eager to deliver your freakiest fetish fantasies,
Disco queen, skirt up the crotch,
Fish-net stockings, bow-legged, anorexic, raisin nipples, tip-toeing
Roppongi on
Stiletto heels.

Yessu, i spikku ingrishhu, i raikku gaijeeen, they kiss you,
hold your hand, open doors for me,
open legs for you, giggling pidgin, covering mouth,
so happy to be
Little YELLOW Slut.

Everybody's seen her:
That Little YELLOW Slut, waiting at
Home, cooking rice, the Japanese
Condoleezza Rice,
Smelling of sushi,
Breath and vagina,
Fish and vinegar,
Fermented rice,
Honored to be

Cleaning lady,
Flight attendant for Singapore Airlines,
Charlie Chan's Angel,
Nurse maid, gardener, Japan-expert's wife,
Mochi manga face,
Yodeling minyo, growling enka,
Sex toy, slant-eyes closed, licking, tasting, swallowing STD semen,
Every drop.

Yessu, i wanna baby who looohkuh gaijeen, double-fold eye,
translucent skin, international school PTA,
maybe grow up to be fashion model, even joshi-ana,
not-not-not happy to be
Little YELLOW Slut.

I recognize her:
That Little YELLOW Slut, rejecting
Japanese, rejected by Japanese,
Ashamed,
Empty inside,
They all look alike,
Faceless, hoping to forget, escape
To America,
Slant-eyed clitoris,
Adopted orphan,
Dream come true for pedophiles,
Serving sake, pouring tea, spilling honey,
Naturalized citizen,
Buying Gucci,
Docile doll,
Rag-doll, Miss Universe, manic harakiri depressive, rape victim,
she is
You, she is me.

Hai, hai, eigo wakarimasen, worship Big Master for mind, matter,
muscle, money, body size correlates to penis size,
waiting to be sexually harassed, so sorry, so many,
so sad to be
Little YELLOW Slut.

A Song for the Big White Bitch

When I was in first grade,
the teacher used
to treat me special
—the only girl in class
with slanted eyes
and yellow skin—
I still
can smell her stuffy perfume, when
she hugged me,
cooing,
"Just like a Chinese doll!"
(she didn't know I was Japanese)
and the praises I got
for speaking even one word
of English—
she didn't know
people were born here
besides the kind like her:
sing a song for
the BIG WHITE BITCH
the curly hair, the powdered flaky face, the
fluttering eyelashes, her soft cries of awe.
the BIG WHITE BITCH
tells me to Revlon my cheeks, crayon my eyes,
Max Factor my lips and color my hair,
the sleek, luring look
in her Maybelline blue eyes,
the soft blond hair,
baby-soft in the breeze,
the sex-appeal teeth—
the larger the eyes, the better,
the deeper into the sockets,
the longer the legs

the whiter the skin, the better.
Suzie Wong and Madame Butterfly
aren't Orientals
but played by whites,
or Nancy Kwan or France Nuyen
(who have white blood in them—very pure—)
Caucasian faces
in Asian masks,
made to please white society,
the BIG WHITE BITCH
with her women's lib
the BIG WHITE BITCH
speaking for the oppressed
(women are the large "minority")
she tells us how to relate to our men
how to control our birth rates
control our sex rates
control our intercourse rates
the BIG WHITE BITCH
relaxes in her couch
emulating Marlene Dietrich or
Miz Scaaawlett O'Hara,
while I scrub her floor
and cook her meals
"Oh—" she exclaims
ever so softly—
"Are Asians so neat
and always so hard-working?"
the BIG WHITE BITCH
the big white busts
the big white haunches
the big white belly
the big dumb blonde
winking
blowing kisses
fainting
sobbing
"Fly me,"
the playmate of the month,

high up on the pedestal
in the glare of the white sun
to be protected
to be embraced
to be kissed on the fingertips
to be frigid in bed
the BIG WHITE BITCH
the Hollywood beauty
Miss USA
Ms USA
with the pink ostrich feathers,
the chic mink coat,
the white diamond ring,
the BIG WHITE BITCH
someday you will be
machine-gunned
with the rest of your kind.

poem Re poet

ninja lost in the commuter train
the voice in the urban wilderness
shaman moaning an improvised chant
the word that kills
the thought that heals
being a poet is being told to take a bungee jump
and the rope is "made in Japan-town"
feeling that fetal taiko-drum beat vibrating from deep within
all the way from my shuddering lips
to my dew-dropping labia folds _ majora and minora
the word that kills
the thought that heals
i don't feel safe:
will the music survive?
standing and sitting and walking and jogging
no different from anybody else
but transforming the everyday into the eternal
adding meaning to the meaningless
connecting with the dead like a radio show
seeing outer space
in the here and now
there is no choice
everywhere
but alone
being a poet
it just happens
the word that kills
the thought that heals

an ode to the Caucasian male

white man
white man
with the silky blond hair
the emerald-blue eyes
and the cool million dollar grin
I won't mind being a Suzy Wong for you.
cuz
I'm tired of the laundry-men
and the dirty restaurant cooks
who can only smell of won ton soup
and talk about chowmein
they don't have the powers,
the style you do
seems you've got to be white
to really be a man
the long sleek legs
with the acid rock walk
in the hot tight pants
where the warm prick dwells
it's okay
you see only the race in me
just a stereotype, not my personality
it's okay
cuz, white man
you have
whiteness
to give.

March Eighth

March Eighth, International Women's Day, was unusually cold that year. Elsie Okada and I huddled close, our hands dug deep into our coat pockets, trying to keep the biting wind out of our collars. The crowd around us filled Union Square, but gave no protection against the wind, which swept through, ignoring the people, finding gaps in between.

"Shit, it is cold." Wisps of white smoke came out in gasps from Elsie's blanched lips.

We stomped on the concrete. I pushed my toes hard. It felt like the pain let the blood circulate in my numbed feet. To keep our legs moving seemed to help. It had been better when we had marched with the Chinatown contingent toward the rally.

"Can you hear what they're saying?" She frowned.

Someone was making a speech, but the amplifying system was so bad it was impossible to make out what was being said. A voice echoed, words running into words, a big vibration in our ears.

"Do you want to move up closer?" I suggested. "We didn't drive for six hours just to freeze."

We made our way through _ long and wild-haired white women holding placards, indicating a union (one of the girls in the Chinatown contingent had told us that the union was elitist, organizing only white and clerical women workers), light-skinned black men selling "The Militant" (when offered the paper, the same women had said, "Nope, I don't agree with your line"), Puerto Rican women with beautiful doe eyes and a beret cocked on their heads (were they from the revisionist PSP?).

Different leaflets were pushed on us, as we moved through the crowd. I took them all with a smile _ CPUSA propaganda, invitations to a benefit dinner to oppose the Chilean fascist regime, appeals to end U.S. aid to Marcos' rule in the Philippines _ and squished them into my knapsack.

We could see the wooden stage now. We were standing among a Latino-looking group, who shouted now and then and cheered. A skinny woman with dark glasses, a miniature Gloria Steinem, was reading from a sheet of paper. Her ash-blonde hair crept down both sides of her face, forming a frame around her white face and dark glasses. Listening carefully, we could pick out her words, "What we need are more women lawyers, more women doctors, more women technicians! We must oppose this male-dominated society!" She paused until some people cheered.

Elsie and I looked at each other, disappointment clearly read in the other's face. Suddenly I felt cold again, and remembered how awkward I felt, when, gathered in the corner of Chinatown, waiting for the march to begin, a woman had asked, "Have you done much study on the Women's Question?" Next to me, Elsie was muttering about tokenism and about how cold she was.

A group of gray coats across the street caught my eye. Their signs read, "Protect the right to life!" "No More Abortions!" Most were old men with hats and scarves around their reddened faces bristled with white and covered with coarse wrinkles. There were some women, though. Their pink scarves and plump white legs stood out in the crowd. Sporadically they screamed out _ something about motherhood and murder. When the men noticed me, one raised his fist, waved it in circles above his head and yelled. I turned my head, trying to catch his words.

But they were different words, a woman's cold sterile voice that I heard. "Just take off your jeans and panties and get up here please." She smiled. She was trying to be kind. Trying to be businesslike, doctor-like, godlike. The smell of the medicine in the air stung my nose, and I felt like crying. I sighed deeply. Might as well get it over with. Taking off one's panties was nothing, right? One did it dutifully before taking a shower, joyously in bed when his eager hand tugged it off, one didn't even think of it when peeing _ no big deal.

But my heart was making queer jerking motions in my throat like a baby chick hopping inside a lighted incubator, and my fingers kept shaking as I undid the zipper on my jeans, doing it fast, not to think about it, yet thinking about it and hesitating and postponing and wishing the ticking of time would goof and let me off. I smiled sheepishly in just my T-shirt. I felt more than naked.

The doctor tried not to notice my embarrassment. Or maybe doing this everyday had actually made her callous. She had put on a gauze mask, so that only her eyes showed emotionless above the white square cloth. I climbed on the examining table and lay down. She told me to put my feet on to the slippers that were attached to the metal poles, which stuck out from the table like thin stiff legs. She drew a white curtain, gently separating the upper part of my body from the lower. Perhaps she was not even out to punish me but was resigned to the fact that Asian women had no morals.

"Mrs. or Ms?" the nurse had asked curtly, as she had filled out my form. Oh, my God, I was thinking. What's happening to me, why is this happening to me, is this really happening to me? As the doctor touched my vagina, my strength eked out of the hole. I put my hands over my eyes.

"The urinal test has shown," the voice over the phone had said, "it is positive."

"OK. Thank you," I had said calmly. I had not cared.

One had to be careful when peeing into the container. When I was in high school, this half-Japanese and half-Filipino guy went around circulating rumors that females did not have control over their peeing as did males. Males could direct their pee anywhere by a flick of a hand, but females couldn't. A lot of guys believed it. It felt silly to be carefully carrying around a test tube of urine. How could they look into the green-yellow liquid and figure out if one was pregnant or not? Did the fetus pee inside of the woman, so that its pee came out, like proof of its existence, along with the woman's pee? Was that why they said that a symptom of pregnancy was an urge to urinate more often?

The doctor had given me an injection and instructed me to count backwards from one hundred _ ninety-nine, ninety-eight, ninety-seven . . .

I was in a dark cave, being pulled by my legs, legs far apart, down the cave, like a product on a conveyor belt. Sometimes I was pulled swiftly, the wind hissing by my ears from the momentum. Fluorescent pink-purple, flashes of black light, jumped at me from hidden corners. A shining purple man with a silk hat, a crazed "daddy-long-legs," limped a weird dance before me, like a crooked Halloween paper skeleton. Machines groaned, its steel jaws digging into the air, crunch-crunching toward my open legs. I was pulled, pulled, down a curving slope turned jet-coaster, a sick feeling falling and rising in my stomach _ the feeling one gets when a elevator stops at a floor. I cried, and I knew I was crying. There was another "me," watching, half-aware of my returning consciousness, yet another part of me dragging me into the fake LSD trip. I kept on calling his name.

It was true, after all, what they put in the corny movies about people calling out their lovers' name in delirium. An annoyed nurse later told me I had disturbed the other patients. I didn't have a lover though. He loved me but didn't love enough. He hadn't understood.

"You don't expect me to go with you to the hospital, do you?"

"No, it's OK. I'll manage."

"Sure, you'll manage."

I had swallowed hard not to choke. He had patted me on the shoulder. He had laughed. Then he had told me of his friends' girlfriends and oh, yeah, even his sister-in-law, who had had abortions and nothing had gone wrong or anything. He had kissed me hard and offered to pay the total costs.

"No, you can just pay half," I had said.

I hated him. I hated his guts. I wanted to castrate him with the sharpest knife and watch him bleed and bleed. I would chop his penis into indistinguishable tiny bits _ chop, chop, chop on the wooden board, with the giant Chinese knife, and cook it nice and brown in the wok and feed it to the dogs. I had loved the same part of him, enveloping it with my lips, cuddling it with my hands, feeling it so nice against my insides. And I was still calling his name.

When my friend in Japan had to have an abortion because of pressures from the guy's mother (they were scheduled to be married soon but not conveniently soon enough, by proper Japanese social standards), her man suggested that they "three" go to their favorite spot on the beach and drown themselves by falling off of a "lover's leap." After the abortion, they still cried together, and he regretted that they hadn't killed themselves. She told all this to me to tell me how serious they were about the baby and about their relationship. Americans would interpret it as a sign of how insane they were and surely of how weak-willed. But there was that perhaps Japanese part of me, wishing (or just playing with the idea, knowing its impossibility), that he had offered to die with me.

Elsie had told me not to take it too hard. She had had an abortion, too. Just think it's a mole or something that has to be scraped off, she had said. But, sometimes, she thought about the baby. Did it look like this? She had put her fingers to her cheeks and made dimples.

She had also waited for me in the waiting room. After her abortion, she had just bled a little, but I had bled until the doctor wanted to insert some machine to look inside of me. I had absolutely refused. Maybe I had gone partially crazy then, maybe my hormones weren't in balance. After all, my insides had been scraped out with a metal rake. Elsie later told me that she had heard clattering noises, pumping noises, whirring, scraping, clanging. Maybe there was a bucketful of blood. Maybe the baby _ or pieces of it _ was floating in it, its fish-eyes looking and not seeing through the film of blood. My uterus _ now I could feel out exactly the formerly mysterious location in my lower abdomen _ had hurt when Elsie's car went over little bumps on the road.

"Do you want to get some coffee?"

I blinked.

"Hey," Elsie tugged at my coat sleeve, "do you want to go get some coffee?"

An Asian woman stood before the podium. Her figure was small, but her voice rang out clear and loud from the speaker. "We are struggling not only against the oppression of women, but in addition against the burden of racism and recognize a basic form of oppression _ that of the masses of working people. We contend that a women's liberation movement should not retain or simply reform the system which exploits and cripples us. True liberation of women can be achieved only by a complete transformation of this inhumane, exploitative system, which breeds on racism and sexism." With her hand, she flipped her long black hair from her shoulder.

"As women, as workers, as oppressed minorities, we must continually fight to secure the right to unionize, decent wages, working conditions, education for our children, health care and day care." Elsie was looking toward the stage. The cold had made her cheeks pink, as though it had slapped her. "World peace can be achieved only when wars of aggression waged by the imperialists of the U.S. and Soviet Union are put to an end. By uniting with the Third World women and men and all working people, we are supporting the struggle for real world peace, for the end of capitalist exploitation, which means the fight for the rights of women, of all working and oppressed people!" The woman turned abruptly and left.

I motioned to Elsie, and we worked our way through the people. I was so cold I was shuddering. My lips would not stop trembling. Elsie pointed out a coffeeshop across the street.

"That speech was good, wasn't it?" an Asian man in his late twenties whom we had marched with from Chinatown, stopped us. His face was pale. He had told us he had not slept at all last night, preparing a leaflet to be distributed that day.

"Yeah," I said.

"It mentioned socialist-imperialism," he said.

I nodded. The penetrating gaze from his gentle narrow eyes made something inside me give a small jump. I was almost afraid of him. "You're driving back to your college today?" he smiled.

"I guess so," Elsie said. I could hear the impatience beneath her tone. We left the short man, standing in his bulky coat, his leaflets piled under his arm. We ran across the street and into the shop, where the warmth tickled our toes and fingers and made our noses run. We sat by the corner and winced when the hot coffee, through the white porcelain, stung our fingers that held the cups. I barely tasted the liquid and merely felt its hotness slither down my throat like a fat snake. I put my warmed fingers next to my cheeks, then put the fingers next to the cup to warm them, then brought them to my cheeks again.

"That speech was good," Elsie was saying, half to herself.

I turned halfway on my revolving chair. By a small table next to the window, a middle-aged white woman was sipping coffee, staring blankly in front of her. She had buttons all over her hat and some on her jacket. There were wrinkled bags beneath her large eyes. Freckles covered her face. I remembered her from the rally. She had yelled something back at the anti-abortion men. Her fingers had over-sized joints and knuckles. She gulped her coffee, and she looked like she was crying. I mused about all sorts of possibilities for her _ marriages, divorces, her jobs (cannery worker, seamstress at a Levi Strauss plant, typist in a "pool"), her children (loved, hated, wanted, unwanted).

Then I remembered perfumed powdered schoolteachers hugging me in their flabby arms, cooing what a nice cute girl I was; that blonde, looking like a TV commercial, who slept with Asian men, believing in their exotic mystical acrobatics; the white spinster superintendent of the cafeteria kitchen, telling me to work faster, Orientals are so lazy, so slow. I searched inside of me for the usual hostility. The woman with the buttons had finished her coffee. She was pulling green and red mittens on her hands. She was small and stout when she stood up. The cold rushed in, like loneliness, when she opened the door and left.

I turned toward Elsie. We would probably drink another cup of coffee and then start driving back.

food for thot

japanese cars must be like sushi, tempura, kaiseki
the designer pontificates at a party
to add value and defy the challenge from hyundai of korea
like yakiniku korean barbecue and bibimbap

think of all the poor people in india
the nun swishing her black habit prays
the chicken soup swimming in the urn turns into urine and the
bread into styrofoam sponge in our throats

let's have a picnic here, mommy, okay?
my son plunks down in the grass
he eats boiled eggs, claiming his place in the japanese family,
believing they are delicious, the best in the world

when will my husband be able to eat again?
my mother asks the doctor, who answers, "never"
after brain surgery, tubes trickle paste through a hole in his stomach
he gurgles in mucus, his eyeballs batty with fright

Cooking Poem

sizzling chopped garlic
minced ginger
neatly cut bok choy
shrieking sesame oil
a giant spoon
tosses
scraping the wok
his arm from behind hugs her stomach
he kisses her ear
"how's your day?"
the shoyu turns greens into black
he tells her the latest occurrences
the spoon bangs
the bok choy
gnarled and wilted
"dinner is ready"
steam from the dish
reaches the ceiling

write it down

write it down
sumi strokes on rice paper
sway over incense
fold origami style and
tie on a tree
write it down
beatings by your father
betrayal by your lover
rapes by your neighbor
scorn from your enemy
write it down
not to remember for legacy
but to purge and purify
not notes for later but
simply to forget
write it down

HAIKU

ステンドグラス
ひかりを染める
妻のゆび

stained glass
nudging color into light
my wife's fingers

春の朝
ピンクが爆発
シフォン舞う

spring morning
pink explodes
chiffon whirls

なき孫が
小皺に霞む
化粧水

dead grandchild
a blurring thought lost in wrinkles
skin lotion's smell

田んぼにも
見える砂漠の
地平線

rice paddies
you can see it
a desert horizon

浜名湖に
沈め忘れる
父の虐待

at Hamanako
forgetting burying
beatings by my father

The Suicide

"I happened to see the old man of the Kimura's today." With that statement, Yoshio began his usual after supper conversation with his wife and, leaning back into his chair, took a sip of his tea. He watched his wife move busily in the small dining room-kitchen area of their company apartment.

He was satisfied with Miyoko as his wife. She worked hard, cooked well. He noted with self-approval that he had judged Miyoko to be the perfect wife as soon as he had seen her round pale face at the "meeting" their parents had arranged. Though he did not like to admit this, he often thought that she was like a mother to him, especially when he would come home drunk late at night. Miyoko would still be up and, after offering him a cold glass of water, would tuck him into the warm futon bed, which she had prepared in advance. Such kindness and what seemed infinite capacity for forgiveness reminded him of his mother.

His thoughts were gently interrupted by Miyoko's small voice. "How was he?" Her quietness was another reason he liked Miyoko. More and more women were losing this virtue, like the ones working in the same company where he worked, who wasted their time, talking and talking, like geese, as a result of what they claimed was liberal Western influence. Yoshio frowned.

Miyoko's fingers looked long and white as they picked up and neatly stacked the bowls, chopsticks and plates. The porcelain clattered lightly as she placed them in the kitchen sink. Yoshio, remembering her question, replied, "Not too well. At first, he didn't even recognize me. I was getting off a bus at the bus stop; he was standing in line to get on. He almost passed by me without looking up."

"His grandson passed away last week." Miyoko's usually downcast eyes looked for a moment directly into Yoshio's. Yoshio found it always difficult to decipher her emotionless glances. They were never challenging though, open and innocent. "I thought I told you."

"I don't remember."

"You were so busy last week." Yoshio knew last week had been as busy a week as any other, but he let Miyoko's effort at saving him from embarrassment pass without any comment.

"His grandson was studying hard for the university entrance exams; wasn't he?" Yoshio drank down his tea. It was lukewarm.

"Oh, that was a long time ago." Miyoko filled a tea pot with water and lighted the gas. "He already got in last year. In fact, into Tokyo University, where you went."

Yoshio looked up. He was remembering his days of studying for the exams. When the world was so quiet and dark outside his study window, he felt as though no one was awake or alive except for himself. He sat before his desk, groaning over memorizing the minutest detail of Japanese history or the subjunctive in the English language, his head and face unbearably hot, his feet and hands numbed by the cold. People were awake, though. Some woman in the neighborhood, who also had a son studying for the exams, would give his mother a sardonic smile when they would meet at the vegetable store. "Every night the lights at your home are on for so long," she would praise, with a half-hidden tone of hostility.

While Yoshio studied, his mother never failed to stay up in another room. She came into his room around two at night with a steaming bowl of noodles for him. When he gulped down the noodles, he vowed he would pass the exams.

He was relieved that he would never have to repeat those times. Many of his classmates had failed, and, unwilling to go to a less prestigious university, had studied for the exams again for the following year. But now that he had graduated and was in Mitsui Corporation, all this seemed remote and, in a way, ridiculous.

"You know, Miyoko, once I experimented how long I could go on studying without stopping, except for going to the bathroom and eating, of course. I lasted for fifteen hours." Miyoko was washing the dishes, so her back was turned, but he could hear her soft laughter. Yoshio picked up the evening paper and started slowly turning the pages. "What was the grandson's name?"

"Mamoru."

"How did he die? Was it an accident?"

Miyoko hesitated, then, "He committed suicide."

Yoshio's fingers on the newspaper froze momentarily, then they made the printed paper crackle a little, lifting a page. Miyoko turned around and spoke quickly. "The mother found him in the morning, and he had cut open his throat. She was crying when she told me. I went to the funeral, and her face was all red and swollen, as though her tears had dried up inside her. And _ she had been so proud of their son. It was like all their hard days were over at last."

Yoshio understood. As soon as one entered a university, life was easy. Most students skipped classes and spent most of their time playing mah-jong and pachinko, joining yacht clubs, going out with the girls, and waiting until their junior year when they got their employment. Failure was rare in a Japanese university, and, if one went to Todai, it was certain that a prestigious corporation would offer employment. Such had been the way Yoshio had passed his Tokyo University days. He had considered it a break between studying for the exams and earning a living in the so-called "real world."

But this Mamoru _ he did not need to kill himself. He did not need to die for shame. He had not failed but succeeded. Yoshio knew of people who killed themselves after failing the exams. Some had failed for the third time. Every year, after the exam period, the newspapers had articles on those who had committed suicide because they had failed. Yoshio personally knew of one _ a high school classmate. The boy, rumors went, had hung himself in the school gymnasium. Yoshio pictured in his imagination the short, quiet youth as a faceless ghost hanging dead in the gym, the image piercing him with a shuddering and strange guilty fear.

The rattling of the tea pot broke the silence. Miyoko quickly reached out, poured the boiling water into a smaller porcelain pot containing the sweet-smelling green leaves. Without looking up from the newspaper, Yoshio stuck out his large cup for his wife to pour the tea. Then Miyoko made a cup for herself and, having sat across from him blew softly upon the liquid to cool it. Yoshio studied her. The hazy steam from the tea rose from her cup as though trying to tickle her nostrils.

She was still gazing into her tea when she spoke, "The mother kept on saying that she wished he had told her everything. What was bothering him so. She kept on repeating that as though that would bring him back." She sighed. Yoshio was not really listening. He casually wondered whether it was what people meant by "maternal instinct" which enabled Miyoko to empathize so deeply with Mamoru's mother.

Yoshio tried to recall this Mamoru. He had been slender and rather unhealthy-looking. He was always facing downward, so that when Yoshio passed him on the streets, the youth's face was hardly visible, hidden behind sloppy hair. A vague shadow, as he walked alone silently in his black school uniform with a leather school bag full of books.

Yoshio saw that Miyoko was looking at him with suddenly serious eyes, "He was thinking too much. People who think too much are never happy."

Yoshio shivered. The woman before him, with that almost bland face, surrounded, encircled by the ocean depth darkness of her hair, with the silent wet eyes and a voice like a murmur, almost like an insect's cry, this woman, whom he thought at time he knew thoroughly _ controlled, possessed _ was suddenly a stranger. She was still looking at him, or seemingly beyond him. "They think about why we live, and they think and think, until there is no answer. Or the answer is that living is dying, and then, they die, making it easy on themselves _ once and for all."

Yoshio breathed in deeply, trying to calm the gradual tremor of his body. His hands were beginning to perspire, and his heart pounded. "Mamoru talked to me one day," Miyoko continued calmly. "He just smiled and asked, why are we women always serving the men, thinking nothing, feeling nothing, while the men go to work, slaving for the 'economic animal.' He said the 'economic animal' isn't really in the Japanese people. But we go on, without thinking. Men go to bars after work, sleep with other women. They don't want to talk to their wives. No one talks or listens."

"Miyoko _" Yoshio found himself calling out.

"It's true, though. We don't think, and, if we did, maybe I'd do what Mamoru did, too. Or, at least, go away, some place far, by myself, and try to find a better way out. Yet then," she smiled faintly, "there may be none. It's like staring deeply into the fire. After a while, one feels one is inside the fire, and one wants to jump in and burn until nothing is left." She paused. "I wake up at night, sometimes, and I get filled with the passion of wanting to die. Everything is so unbearable. Except dying _ "

"Didn't you hear? I told you to stop." Yoshio had half-risen. His fists were clenched on the table, shaking it slightly. Miyoko was facing him. He wanted to hit her. His teeth were biting into each other. "That is all nonsense." Hearing himself, he was pleased with the sound of his voice _ so self-composed, so authoritative. He eased the tension in his muscles. He tried not to look at his wife. "There are confused people in this world. But we, as proper Japanese, must live respectably. I have a good job, I work hard and I bring home a good salary. I will keep on getting promoted, and you will have an even easier life than you lead now. I'm doing this all," Yoshio swallowed and went on, "I'm doing this all for you. You have no reason to complain."

He did not expect any reply. He stole a glimpse toward Miyoko from the corner of his eye. Her face was downcast and he could not see her expression. He wondered if she was crying and smiled to himself, hoping that she was. Yoshio forced a kindness into his tone, "I understand you were upset by the boy's death. Just never mention Mamoru or any of that talk again; do you understand?"

Miyoko stood up next to Yoshio and faced him. She was small. Her hair cast a shadow over her face, a moon waning crescent. She smiled and nodded, "I understand. Would you like some tea?" As she turned, Yoshio struggled, trying to erase the doubt within his mind. Instead, he eyed her thin waist as she stooped to fill the pot with water.

Ara-Saa (Short for "Around Thirty" in Japanese)

around thirty
you've turned the corner
past your expiration date
still looking for mr right
clinging to a sex in the city view on life
strutting the career highway on jimmy choos
while your market value drops
a chloe bag on an outlet rack
there's no space, get real,
between the cute nymphomaniac teen and
the victorious pregnant housewife
except for trips to massage salons
giggly ethnic dinners out with the girls
nowhere affairs with the married boss
stop wondering why
no one good asks you out
stop asking why
no one notices
you're smart, beautiful, on-the-go,
in top notch belly-dancing-lessons shape
and ever so available
life is not a yahoo auction
life is not a disneyland make-a-wish-list
you must stop
and ask yourself
how you can become
that person
who can love
without asking
for
anything
back
in return

A poem for Winchester Nii Tete, a young but master percussionist

fingertips
that moment
sound spills
bouncing bubbles of invisible gems
exploding softly from warm antelope skin
sparkling
through the dark air
fragrance of a forgotten African flower
roosters, stripes in squares,
spilling on rolls of fabric unfolding
black on Kandinsky beige,
red on blue,
sound
unseen but seen
no mistake
inside
full
complete
in a single stroke
understanding all
generations and generations speak
sound
simply
by your touch

Vertigo

my head is swaying though it's deadly still
red blood plasma swimming wildly
my brain rotting like miso
around and around
my feet don't touch the ground
the walls swoop sideways
in time to a Satie piano
the pale ceiling darkens
turning upside down
i must be having a stroke
i must have a brain tumor
hormones going berserk
vagina drying
bad breath stale body odor of fungus
graying hair thinning
even eyelashes thinning
but fat getting fatter
you got to be kidding
dizzy biological clock ticks to the grave
reproductive function grinds to a halt
fossils of dinosaurs sleeping inside the earth
no more monthly blood
no more monthly mood swings
just permanent depression and deprivation
instinct of species preservation
menopause, people say,
marks a step into a more spiritual stage in life
the best years
the final
best years
but the top of my head is filled with air
and deep down, the fiery hotness,
where the flashes come,

that spot where the root of the umbilical cord
a tiny amputated limb
awaits
inside
makes me masturbate in my bed

Asian American Art Story

A summer night _ cool though from the ocean breeze and the fog that, like a moving smoking mountain, merges avenue by descending numbered avenue, all the way to San Francisco's Japantown.

I'm already feeling pretty good from the cheap Chablis. I know even my skin stinks with alcohol. I'm in good shape, this being some years ago. My one bare shoulder is brown and shiny.

I'm in my gypsy-look stage so I'm wearing a big soft white top _ a little satiny _ that hangs lopsided off the shoulder and a bigger skirt that's mostly black with a neon yet kimono-like chrysanthemum print _ an attempt to maintain the Japanese ethnicity in my apparel; another being the jangling earrings, silver, that are molded into the shape of fans. A thick purple sash with pink and gold tassels encircles a thin waist that's never experienced pregnancy beyond six weeks.

I'm standing with most of my weight on my left leg and a wrist cocked on a hip, because it's nearing eight o'clock, the time the reading's supposed to start, and no other poet from our workshop has shown up, except for myself and Pacifico, who's settled himself down next to the wine jug and already looks so dazed I'm afraid he won't make it to the microphone. The technician from the city's arts program has, thank god, shown up, and is busy setting up, tripping over the black snake-like cords and going, "Testing, testing," into the phallic mikes.

On second thought, maybe it'd be better if no one shows up at all. There's always a few _ I see familiar faces now, peering into the dark seating area; one waves to me; I nod _ so readings end up resembling a wake for some distant relative _ sad but not overwhelming, just enough to leave an unpleasant aftertaste.

The one who waved walks up to me. "Nervous?" she asks, flipping her black hair over her shoulder. The silk strands fall together like a curtain.

I shake my head. "How come nobody's responsible enough to be on time for these gigs? I always get stuck holding the bag."

"No one's here anyway," she points out, meaning to be comforting.

"Thanks."

"They'll come. There's an understanding, you know. We all operate on Colored People's Time. You're being crazy expecting everyone to be here on time, Misty," she nudges my elbow. "See? Here's Dan Yamaguchi, armed with his pile of right-on poems."

I turn and see Dan, sure enough carrying a worn out folder under an arm that's in a worn out work-shirt. The layered ends of his hair rustle at his shoulders. I smile, but naturally he ignores me and moves toward Pacifico, near the wine. I watch Dan pouring himself a cup and Dan and Pacifico exchanging the power handshake and slapping each other on the back, saying stuff like, "What's up bro?" "The same, man," or whatever, and I feel a slight nausea in my diaphragm.

"What about the lights?" the tech is asking me. They're always asking me as though I should know.

"I don't know."

The Chinese American tech's face visibly expresses disgust. Poor guy. He has the thankless job of teching for all these untogether community groups. I don't blame him.

"Well, can you just leave that center area lit, sorta in general, for the whole thing?" I suggest, trying to be helpful.

He still looks disgusted but runs up to the tech booth, plays with some switches and calls down if that's what I want.

"Fantastic. Fine, fine," I say. "Thanks." I feel that I'm going against my feminist principles, but, when he comes down, I hug the tech, demonstrating my gratitude by letting his arm push against the softness of my breast, and he looks a lot less disgusted. Maybe he'll do his job right, while he's here. The extent I have to put myself out for this workshop when no one else seems to give a fuck.

I was the one who had typed out the press releases, Xeroxed them, folded them, stapled them, stamped our bulk-rate nonprofit organization stamp, and delivered the pack to the post office. I was the one who'd attempted to design the poster, but it looked so awful, I had to go Barnaby Kim, and I had to bring him the grass, out of my own pocket, to help urge him to contribute his talents for this worthy literary cause. I was the one who traversed what felt like every corner of San Francisco, risking my life on the infamous twenty-two MUNI bus rides, to tape Barnaby's silkscreen posters advertising this memorable event, to occur, I glance at my watch, excuse me, to have occurred, beginning two minutes ago.

To confess, it wasn't that bad. Sheryl helped me a lot. And I look at my friend with the long hair, standing before me, in her skin tight jade dress and black stockings and heels. "What are you going to read?" she asks lazily. "Not that it matters. The audience is only going to be your friends, who'll forgive you for anything." With another one of her supposedly soothing remarks, she slides away into the darkness to find a seat.

"Tell me when you folks are ready to start," the tech instructs me, his tone taking a slight friendliness.

By the stage is a cluster of people, wearing Army jackets, paint-speckled overalls and Hawaiian shirts that have long lost their impact in color. They are studying type-written sheets with rather uptight concentration. I sigh with relief that everyone's here.

"When do we go on?" a voice interrupts my thoughts. His thinly elongated Japanese eyes are barely visible behind the thick wire-rimmed glasses and masses of hair that connect into a moustache and beard below. The only discernible flesh are the nose and the pinkish lips, and, boy, can he blow that saxophone with those lips _ the reason I hired his trio for our performance, fighting some objections from the group that our grant money could be put to better use than feeding some bum musicians.

Let's give credit where due, though. These musicians showed up over an hour early, laid out their equipment, did a quick sound check with the tech and had lots of time left over, to grab something to eat, if they'd wanted, before the poets trickled in.

"Six poets are scheduled to read tonight, so three will read, then music, then three more; how's that?"

"Sounds good," he says.

I wish I'd kept my mouth shut because now everyone's going to blame me for dictatorially and dogmatically deciding the program, without taking a democratic vote or anything. But, damn it, we're going on any second; how can they expect me to hold a meeting?

Too late, now. It's not my fault. Everyone asks me because either no one else is there or else whoever's there's too drunk or spaced out to take control.

The saxophone player walks off to tell the rest of the group. And I follow his gait, not because I'm interested in him but because I want to see the guy on the guitar. He's very quiet and always stooped over his guitar, even while they're waiting around so you can't see his cute face, and I wish he'd look up when the saxophone player talks to them, and he does, and I think I'm going to melt on the spot, I mean, all my juices seeping from my vagina and my bones turning to hot wax, starting from pelvis on out.

He has a skimpy undershirt on, very sexy; his muscles are right without being overly bulging and masculine _ just the way I like them _ and what's sexier are his straight-legged jeans (Lee, I remember), an old pair, nothing to it, except his ass is _ his ass is _ is _ superb. You know what I mean. The way some men are into legs or tits, women are the same. Personally, I'm open. It might be a neck I notice or a sinew on an arm. With him it was his ass; OK?

He's turning around to place his guitar in his case, and there is _ his cutest ass _ and I dream it's me, not the Fender Stratocaster, he's laying, so gently, into the red velour of his bed, I mean, case.

"Let's start." It's Dan Yamaguchi, and he's got the nerve to sound impatient and irritated, as though he's the one who's done all the work, and I've kept *them* waiting. Jesus!

I usually have a good time when I read. Or rather I make it a point to have a good time. No one's really listening so might as well. Besides it's my Baby going out there _ my poems, my Baby. Why make it all any more like a funeral than it has to be? I respect my work for the simple reason that no one else does. No one's going to come pat me on my back, except for the horny guys who mistake a woman's reading an erotic poem for an open invitation to the world for a slumber party in her bed. "I'm interested in lending a hand to get your work published," is the come on, aimed to be lethal. Sad; huh? Even "What's your sign?" beats that.

I have this friend who's basically extremely bitter, something to do with growing up in a Japanese American farming community in California and having a suppressed father who acted like his family were invisible, instead of acting like those middle class American fathers, like the one Beaver Cleaver had. And the

Japanese American Nisei mother _ that's another long story, but, in short, she's not like Beaver's mom either.

Anyway, this friend used to say _ more than once, during our midnight sessions over chamomile tea _ that she could've been a dancer if only her parents had given her the chance while young, because she had the inborn talent, except now, in her mid-twenties, it's too late, even if she's taking two classes a night after work. Her parents used to laugh at her when she'd tap dance on their porch steps, pretending to be a Mouseketeer. Worse, they taught her to be ashamed. She wasn't even supposed to be angry, let alone artistic. She was supposed to maintain a constantly stoic Noh mask of proper Japanese serenity and submissiveness.

I keep going off on tangents about this friend, but, as I said, she's very bitter. She'd spit that artists are in it for their power, to be in the limelight, to bask in their glory. What power? What glory? This filthy stage that hasn't been swept in weeks? Really, I'd hate to be a dancer and have to do a move like slither on this floor and get up with year-old gum and cobwebs on my leotard.

She doesn't understand. No one does.

We do it for the love of it.

It's the faith of believing in the unbelievable.

There are much easier ways to make money than getting fifteen dollars for a poem published in some obscure small press offset job, courtesy of some arts council, or five dollars for being a runner-up in a local fiction contest.

I write because I live to write and write to live. And poetry pulsates in my blood _ which reminds me, in an offhand kind of way _ I better catch that guitarist before he takes off. I'm searching in the crowd for the Lee jeans ass.

I see him. He's laughing. He must be a little drunk. His wine cup dangerously tips in his hand. He's standing with three or four guys _ being very mellow and community.

I dig out the already signed checks from my huge cloth bag ("The bag's bigger than you," guys would tease me, assuming that they were being clever and inspired) and distribute each check to each mellow, community musician, saving the one for the ass till the last.

I'm not a bit nervous when I approach him. I don't reach out and grab his ass, a distinct possibility. I hand him the check with one hand and place the other casually on his shoulder _ merely a cordial gesture. My advice: Be cautious with Asian men. They have a tendency to be easily intimidated by aggressive women, even gorgeous ones.

"Are you gay? My friend says you're too cute to be straight," I whisper into his ear, practically licking his lobe, knowing damned well he's heterosexual. Otherwise, you might get whacked in the face. After all, this is San Francisco. Actually, I'm thinking my come on is inspired and clever. I'm asking him if he's available in a way that's flattering and slightly offbeat. No? Maybe it *was* a dumb thing to say. Who cares? It worked.

This story could end here. A crazy girl who's convinced herself she's a poet _ synonymous with viewing herself as a prophet, goddess, witch and nymph ("nymphomaniac," my enemies would sneer, but skip that) (some would also say, "revolutionary," but skip that, too) _ this madwoman meets sensitive, good-looking, creative gentleman, musically inclined, endowed with quality equipment of inorganic and organic specimen, open to working on a relationship, possibly a commitment, meanwhile offering fun and crazy times together. Wonderful story, n'est-ce pas? Except we Japanese say, "Ne?"

But it doesn't end here. My story, of course, goes on and on, I suppose, until death, and I'm not dead yet, but I don't mean it that way. This story has a really nasty ending.

What I mean is, all of a sudden, I get this queer letter in the mail, signed by Dan Yamaguchi, for an emergency meeting for the workshop. I don't pay much attention to it, when I open the envelope, except to mark it in my calendar, next Tuesday night at seven-thirty at the workshop, because just then my lover pulls me close to his smell. The smell of sweat and skin and mouth and hair _ like tasting seaweed on your tongue, feeling wet sand in between your fingers, hearing the fog horn go off, echoing inside your brain, till you're gone, gone, gone.

As soon as I get to the meeting, I sense something is wrong. First of all, there're too many people. The dingy room is half-filled with cigarette smoke. I'm only ten minutes late, but every workshop member is present, probably the only meeting with perfect attendance in the history of the workshop. I sit on the broken down sofa and smile at no one in particular. Maybe it's paranoia but everyone is critically eyeing my leather pants, perhaps as an indication of my decadent bourgeois ways? My intuition, unfortunately, is pretty much on target, as it turns out, because, sooner or later, the discussion moves in that direction.

When I just sit down, however, I couldn't pretend to fantasize what was coming. I tap Pacifico's arm, ask him for a cigarette. He happens to be sitting next to me. He shakes his box, waits till I choose a cigarette, then lights a match for me, cups the flame with his brown hands that are unexpectedly delicate for his solid build. I should have read the pity in his eyes, the guilt in his manner, as he watched the innocent and stupid lamb prancing up to the sacrificial altar, in her leather pants and cleavage-revealing purple blouse.

I blow the smoke toward the cracks in the ceiling and try not to notice the silence as though everyone were holding their breaths to hear the metallic clanging of my earrings, all those Asian eyes on me, like alley cat tigers out for the kill. I also try to block out the fact that community cadre-types are sitting in the room, the vaguely recognizable faces of those perpetually hanging out in J-town, with their red, always red, splattered leaflets and newspapers. They've certainly never been members of our poetry workshop.

"We've been in existence for nearly two years now, and I called this meeting to have an opportunity to reflect upon our past activities and especially to talk about the direction we'd like to be heading in the future. It's my feeling that, some time during the course of the workshop's development, we may have lost sight of our original goals and values, which centered on our work for the community."

That is Dan Yamaguchi talking, and I have to pinch myself almost, not to tune out. By now, I'm catching on that I, Misty Mandai, this nymph, prophet, goddess, poet, witch may have walked right into a Salem hunt.

"There are certain members in the workshop that have taken over the leadership," here, he stares right at me, then continues, facing the crowd, "and I question that leadership. Where it's taking us. In light of our goals that we set up as a group earlier."

There are some comments from the floor. A couple of guys aren't hip yet to what's happening and are making random remarks about the workshop goals, the community and what have you, and Dan lets them voice their off-the-wall viewpoints, for he knows there's no hurry. No one's going to come to my aid. Not even the ones who like me.

The cadres speak up now with their practiced rhetoric. They emphasize Dan's points in an attempt to bring the flow of the meeting back to the main purpose _ purging me. Dan speaks again, "In the beginning, we were formed to serve the community. Now, certain people are saying, we can write whatever we want because, hey, we're community, too. There has to be a line drawn somewhere as to what's politically correct and what's politically incorrect."

People are nodding, looking serious and impressed.

"Bullshit!" I say, and my voice is trembling. For once, I hate being in a room full of Asian men. (The women are there, but are few and silent, and they, too, stare at my leather pants, not bothering to disguise their disdain.) I feel weak, being a woman, and I am afraid. "How do you draw the line? Who's to say? That a poem with barbed wires is a correct poem because it refers to the Internment camps, but a poem about loving a man isn't because loving a man isn't a Japanese American experience? Do we have to have 'ojiichan' and 'obaachan' in our poems to make them valid? I'm sick of all this." My words come out fast, shaking and tumbling, one after the other.

I touch Pacifico's arm to ask for another cigarette, and he jumps. He hands me the cigarette but won't light it for me. I have to fumble in my big bag for my lighter and while at it, wish I could climb in there and hide, burying my head among my cosmetics and cry. But I guess I appear strong and calm from the outside. That's what I've been told.

"You guys don't even know your Marx and Lenin backwards or forwards and you're throwing all this dogmatic shit down. It's just going to hold us back. We're still in our formative stage. We have to try everything. Take risks and experiment." I cross my leather legs. Subconsciously, I admire my pants. They are beautiful, and they were cheap. Fifty percent off sale.

I'm thinking about the joy of having purchased my pants because what I'm forced to confront right now is too horrible. I am hurt.

"Speaking of dogmatic," Dan focuses his gaze right into my eyes, freezes it there, "I didn't think that was right, the way you handled that last reading."

Here it comes out.

I'm too numb to be hurt.

They're saying totally weird shit, now _ that I'm writing for the white mainstream, the worst insult attributable to a non-white poet; that my poems aren't fit to wrap Chinatown fish in; that I'm ego-tripping, probably praying I'd make it on to the Tonight Show, one particularly malicious cadre-type jeers.

I'm happy he's home when I get back. He has Jimi Hendrix on full blast, and he's playing the solo, note for note, along with the record. I wait by the threshold. He notices me and puckers up his mouth, stoops over suddenly, magically running his fingers over the guitar neck, up and down, up and down, and then leans back, arching his spine, his face pinched in pain, as his guitar wails then groans. He smiles what he thinks is a devastating smile any groupie would swoon over, wiggles his hips a bit. That last move makes me smile _ a bit.

He reaches over, unplugs the amplifier. "Hi, baby. How'd the meeting go?"

I shrug.

He comes over and kisses me. My hand on his naked back contacts beads of perspiration. With my fingertips, I trace the groove on his skin, left by the strap of his instrument. His lips taste salty. I want to tell him everything, pour it all out, but there's too much to say.

"Hendrix was a genius," he mumbles with his eyes closed. "Did I tell you I went to the same high school as did Jimi Hendrix?" He grew up in Seattle.

"What is Asian American art?" I speak into his mouth, and our teeth bump.

"Hell if I know," he says.

Just then, some birds take off from the tree that's right outside our window, and their wings flap the air, energized with a desperate vibration.

Doves _ we'd started to call them, even though they are just dirty pigeons from Golden Gate Park.

I start to open my mouth, but he places a callused finger. "Shhh . . ." He waits till the last sound of the birds fades, and he lights a candle that's stuck in an empty plastic orange juice bottle, and then turns off the light switch. The shadow of his plants looms larger than life, growing jungles on the walls and ceiling.

For Cher

last night
in stained lights of a
boogie oogie oogie disco
you showed me typed in red
your fiery poetry about
your Manila legend price
his chocolate smooth skin
Pacific passionate sea whispers
his sensual moves
and non-moves
when he stops;
poetry
is caught
in your long long Korean silk hair
your mind
toy kazaguruma windmills children hold at omatsuri
tinsel colors that twirl whirl
like lovers' fantasies
like hidden immigrant dreams
your opaline eyes larger than your rings
transparent white skin on arms your love keeps rubbing
your nights when loneliness is not in bed;
love sisterly
though
is always here
to cry with you when our faces blend invisible in the dark
as we laugh together sharing pains that sound too alike;
who else _ beautiful Cher _ would talk of
mono no aware
at Eppamanados/serious look/sitting sipping
holding a Black Russian?

Ron Tanaka Cooks Rice

Ron Tanaka
creates poems
waiting for the rice to cook

Hearing but not listening to the
muttering bubbles
"koto koto butsu butsu"

The glue rising overflows with the steam
pushing open a crack in the lid
sticks to the rim

Floats in the air
surrounds him writing in his cashmere sweater
diaphanous fog

He is stooped over his kitchen table
where his favorite shino wares are lined
white but shibui luminescence

Roses do not bloom on his page
only irises, water reeds, gold chrysanthemums
They are burned when they wilt

"Ah!" he shouts, half English, half Japanese, mostly Sansei
He rushes to the stove, turns down the heat,
sniffing to make sure

The gohan will be perfect
each grain sparkling
"Gochisousama deshita," his daughter will say when she's done

Thank you for the wonderful meal

The Nunnery

With a harsh tug, Theresa Okamura pulled Magdeleine Saito into the closet.

"Terry, we'll be late for Friday Mass," Magdeleine protested. The mops and brooms towered over her.

"Oh, so what?"

Theresa's face was almost invisible, surrounded, under a gauze veil, by her neatly cropped hair, as an acorn is by its cap.

"Fuck Mass."

She threw out the words as though testing their irreverence against a non-existent listener.

Magdeleine could smell the chalk dust and the dryness of dirt with Theresa's overly sugary breath and the grime caught under her fingernails as Theresa slowly, with one hand, embraced Magdeleine's shoulder and, with the other, began fumbling under Magdeleine's starched school uniform blouse.

The fingers found her still half developed left breast. They stroked the smoothness. Then her palm rubbed the nipple, which bent, without hardening, back and forth to the hand's movements.

Silently, Magdeleine allowed Theresa to proceed with this, now almost daily ritual.

Theresa's other hand edged down from the shoulders, caressed the hips over the checkered navy blue skirt, and swept under the skirt, against the bare thighs that reacted with goose flesh, spreading into the knee socks.

When the hand approached her panties, Magdeleine gasped, "Don't, Terry."

The hand stopped. The other hand moved to the right breast and squeezed it roughly.

"Why not?" Theresa's hand at Magdeleine's crotch began sliding into the downs of her pubic hair.

Magdeleine jerked away.

"Please. You know I love you."

"Then why not?" Theresa's brown eyes peered innocently into Magdeleine's. Theresa switched into Japanese, "Iijanai. There's nothing wrong."

"But, down there, it's different," Magdeleine replied in Japanese. "It's more private." She said the word, "private," in English.

They emerged from the closet, blinking at the sudden brightness of the dank school corridor. Magdeleine giggled when she saw that Theresa's veil was half-covering her face. They adjusted their veils, took out their white cotton gloves from their skirt pockets.

"Hurry," Theresa said in Japanese.

In their shared embarrassment, they both began to laugh hysterically. Magdeleine's pale skin flushed. She put a gloved hand over her lips to stifle her chuckles.

"Girls!"

The voice from behind made them jump. To their eyes, it was the nun's black habit, an ominous silhouette, and not the Caucasian woman, that was stalking briskly up the hallway. The wooden beads of her rosary jingled, and her laced black boot-like shoes squeaked to the mechanical rhythm of her steps.

"You sinners, why are you both not at Mass?" she said, stopping several paces before them and glared at the two downcast figures. "And how many times do I have to remind you not to speak Japanese in school?"

Her British accent emphasized the sternness of her tone. The nun continued, "Your parents are sending you to an expensive missionary school because they want you to learn English."

She let out a low satirical laugh that was not real laughter.

"That's not the reason you don't want us to speak Japanese," Theresa wanted to say. "It's because you can't understand what we're saying. You're in our country for so many years, yet you haven't bothered to learn our language."

She could not say any of these words _ words which, ironically she did not notice, she was thinking in English. Instead, she bit her bottom lip.

The two did not dare even give a side glance to each other.

"Well," the older woman sighed with irritation, "instead of going to Mass, I suggest both of you go back to the study hall and write out, in ink, one hundred times, 'I shall not be late to Mass.' I shall be with you in a minute."

The nun studied them, as though waiting for an answer.

To prevent herself from shaking nervously, Theresa had been fixing her gaze on one of the dark lines in between the marble on the floor. The nun's anticipating silence caused her to look up. She observed absent-mindedly that the nun's face appeared separated from the rest of her body. The body portion was completely covered in black. A veil, also black, draped over the head portion, reaching the waist. A crepe-like cloth, outlining the face, and a white band across the forehead, made the face look shrunken, suspended weirdly above a tiny but conspicuous speck of wrinkled skin showing between a narrow white collar and black veil.

Theresa quickly averted her eyes. She focused on the large cross that hung against the woman's flat chest. The figure of Christ was stuck, limp, dead, almost lopsided, on the metal.

"I'm sorry, Sister," Theresa offered in a monotone. Speaking allowed her to catch a glimpse of her friend next to her. She realized, with a little surprise, that Magdeleine had been audibly crying.

"Hurry up, now," the nun chided.

The girls hastened down the corridor.

"Don't run, girls!" she called after them.

A solitary window at the end of the dim hall illuminated a reproduction of a life-size medieval painting of the Virgin Mary depicted as a young girl, perhaps a teen-ager. The nuns were fond of lecturing that the image of Mary embodied the purity, femininity and beauty toward which the girls were to strive.

Every year, the school celebrated the Immaculate Conception with the entire student body's singing in a long procession that began in the main corridor, marched to the chapel for the service, then ended up before a curtained stage in the assembly room. Each student had been handed an old artificial lily, which was stored in a cardboard box for the rest of the year.

In rows of seven, the girls went to the bottom of the stage and solemnly stuck the flower in a painted green wooden box, reciting, in unison, the line, "I give you the lily of my heart."

After this ritual was completed, the curtain was ceremoniously drawn, to reveal a flesh and blood replica of the painting. The most favored student of the Senior class was chosen in advance by the nuns to sit in the same outlandish pink costume of the picture, the head cocked slightly to the left, eyes downcast toward folded hands on her lap, to sit in the privileged role as the Mother of God.

As the day of the festival drew near, the girls whispered among themselves about who was going to get picked that year. The members of the Senior class tried to behave extra obediently to impress the nuns in order to win the much sought after honor. But both Theresa and Magdeleine knew subconsciously that certain girls, whether they liked to admit it or not, were, by definition, ousted from candidacy. The painting surely depicted a young girl, but the Virgin was blond.

Magdeleine and Theresa entered the study, the last door on the corridor. By then, Magdeleine had stopped weeping. They headed toward their desks, which were a couple of rows and many desks apart.

In the back of the study room, another nun was running the Xerox machine. She was having difficulty and, in frustrated French, was begging the machine to work properly.

"Bonjour, Sister." Magdeleine bowed to the nun.

Theresa repeated the greeting, but the old woman, absorbed in her efforts, barely acknowledged them. Magdeleine whispered to Theresa whether they should help, but Theresa shook her head. The other nun might come in, any minute.

They sat before their wooden desks, opened the tops, took out pieces of paper and fountain pens, and, sighing deeply, began to write out the words.

Theresa played with the idea of utilizing "an assembly line method" of writing out vertically the first word, "I," for one hundred times, then the second word, "shall," for another one hundred times, and so on, until the sentences were constructed, more routinely, piece by piece. She quickly decided against the thought. Since the two were the only ones being punished, she would be spotted immediately.

She wrote out the first sentence on the top line, then went to the next line. After a while, she became almost hypnotically engrossed in the task, wishing desperately, without any logical reason, to finish in as little time as possible. She could scarcely hear the despairing cries of the French nun, conversing with the Xerox machine. She could only hear the repetitive scratching of her pen tip against the paper. Theresa had to be careful, though, not to write too rapidly because her script would become sloppy. Then the nun would force her to do it again.

Theresa heard the heavy study door opening, then the rosary, the leather squeaks, the swish of the veil and habit.

Theresa sensed the fermented odor of the nun, walking toward her desk, not stopping, but checking her work, walking on, toward the back of the study, and, ignoring the French nun, around the last desk, to the other row, to Magdeleine's desk.

For a moment, Theresa wanted to scream. She wanted to run to her friend. A hotness inside her abdomen, like pre-menstrual fever, the urge to protect Magdeleine from the nun, seized her, though she was not sure how or even why. To her relief, the nun's consistent steps continued on, past Magdeleine, and led to the front of the study. Then she heard the screeching of a chair being drawn back as the nun seated herself before the large desk, placed on a slightly elevated platform.

Theresa's hand, especially the bottom of her thumb and her two smallest unused fingers, gradually became cramped from writing. The callus on her index finger was red beneath the stained blue of the leaking ink. Her neat script flowed from her pen, a liquid vein on the page, until it became dried blue words, lined across the paper _ identical, on top of each other _ like the uniformed students, seated at the study hall; or every one of them, kneeling, with a simultaneous thump, echoing upward to the cavernous chapel ceiling, then crossing themselves in one automatic motion, "In the Name of the Father, the Son and the Holy Ghost _ Amen;" running out of the stone building together, laughing, during recreation period; singing with high-pitched angel choir voices, "Ave Maria" in procession.

Footsteps from the corridor indicated that the other students were returning from Mass. Theresa kept on writing. She saw by the numerals she had written in the left hand margin that she was still on her seventy-seventh sentence. She did not wish to see the other students give each other knowing eye signals, raise their shoulders in contempt. Desks opened and shut with polite bangs.

About her eighty-third sentence, the nun rang a small bell from the platform. At the tinkle, the students rose to their feet at once and single-filed out of the study, leaving Magdeleine and Theresa at their desks.

"Theresa and Magdeleine," the nun spoke after the room fell silent, for the other nun had completed her Xeroxing. "You may come to the refectory after you finish. Leave your papers on my desk."

"Yes, Sister," they replied.

Theresa watched the nun step down from the platform, walk toward the door and leave. After waiting a few minutes to confirm her absence, she turned her head. Magdeleine's long coarse hair was spilled over her desk.

"Maggie." Her whisper sounded like a hiss in the large room. She vocalized more normally, "Maggie."

Magdeleine's eyes had a stunned expression as though startled from a dream.

"Are you finished?"

"Just about. How many more do you have?"

"Ten or so."

"Let's get it over with."

"Okay."

Theresa's hand felt lighter. Finishing first, Magdeleine came and sat on Theresa's desk. She watched her hand's writing, seeing, from upside down, a meaningless pattern of ink.

"Maggie, let's go to the convent." Theresa had not lifted her head.

Magdeleine was caught breathless by the suggestion. Theresa stood up energetically, stacked her papers under one arm and carelessly threw her pen inside her desk. "Do you want to?" She looked directly at Magdeleine, then went to put the papers on the nun's desk. Magdeleine followed Theresa and placed her papers next to Theresa's.

"I don't know," Magdeleine mumbled. "We have to go to lunch."

"They won't miss us." She prodded the other girl's elbow. "Ne, ikoo yo. Let's go."

Magdeleine broke into a smile and nodded.

Their shoulders bumped into each other as they went past the painting in the corridor. The hallway bent into a staircase.

They ran up two flights, panting in excitement. The patter of their sponge-soled school shoes echoed in the empty corridor, down another staircase and exited to a small courtyard. They stooped their backs a little, running by the bushes, holding their breaths, not to start giggling, when they could hear, through the refectory window, the girlish voices chanting their grace before the meal. The glass shook gently with the singsong of the undistinguishable words. They reached the other side of the courtyard, opened the door to the chapel.

"Wait, Terry." Magdeleine caught Theresa's sleeve. It felt wet beneath the armpit. "Someone might be in there."

"But this is the shortest way."

Magdeleine began to tremble.

"Maggie, do you want to go to the refectory? You can, you know."

Magdeleine felt her eyes smart at the disdain in Theresa's tone. But her heart thumped against her chest, against her whole external body from the inside, until her ears hurt, as though they would erupt, spurting a discharge of blood and pus.

"Terry," she pleaded.

"No one will see us. They'd be too busy praying." Theresa shrugged.

Magdeleine feebly returned Theresa's smile. She grabbed for Theresa's hand, as they entered the coolness of the chapel hallway. They walked as quickly as they could without making too much noise, past the marble basin of Holy Water, the two doors leading into the chapel, from which effused the smell of candles, a smell, Theresa often thought, like that of burning honey.

As soon as they came out of the chapel, they sped across to the convent building.

"Was anybody there?" Magdeleine asked in between breaths.

"I didn't look."

Once in the convent, they hesitated. Now in unexplored territory, they did not know in which direction to go.

"Do you know the joke about what fun the priest has?" Theresa relaxed her grip.

"Yeah," Magdeleine laughed. "Nun."

Theresa wiped her hand against her skirt. They wandered through the hall and paused before an open door. The small room was starkly empty, except for two bunk beds with grayish white sheets. The whole room _ its floor and walls, even the window _ reflected a gray hue. Too afraid to venture in, they walked on passing some more doors, mostly closed.

"Let's go back," Theresa remarked with a bored finality.

Magdeleine did not reply. She was staring at a door, larger and heavier than the others. Magdeleine, slipping an arm around Theresa's, pulled her.

"What are you doing, Maggie?"

They had to tiptoe to peek in through the small window on the door. Magdeleine strained her eyes into the darkness. The room was small. Finally, her slowly dilating pupils detected a black form against the wall.

It was a nun's habit _ hanging, because it seemed to sway very slightly, but with an inhuman lack of control. Was it on a clothes hanger?

Then she saw its eyes, large glowing balls, like two dull light bulbs _ no, more with the uneven glitter of the dying embers of coal.

She shrieked, for she saw, behind them a shriveled mummified hide, drooping into the shadow of the habit.

She heard Theresa's scream.

And they both stumbled down the hallway, banging into each other. They ran into the sunlight and did not stop until they were far enough into the playground so the convent walls were lost behind the trees.

"Did you see?" Magdeleine heard herself stuttering.

Instead of answering, Theresa made Magdeleine sit on the grass beneath the trees and gently but confidently lifted Magdeleine's skirt, to reveal white flesh, showing, close beneath the surface, purple veins crawling up the widespread thighs.

Demon Worship

to my touch
he is surface soft textured
hardened jade within

"you have a nice one," I say
the first night we meet

he is always awake
probably blind
in perpetual erection
thinking no thoughts
having no conscience
Monk piano move-
ments
fitting
so perfectly
my internal space of stars

violent instinctual
animal of music
quick pacedly
choking a uterus
multiple tight till
it gives up
coming
any more

his churning
jazz rolls
lips outlining shape
wetness tonguing form
fill
my mouth
with warm sweetness
that I drink in

like our love

Disco Chinatown

street blood throbbing
punk maggots of the slums with fake IDs
smelling British Sterling
cover the stink of sweat, car grease and dirt
and the blood from being cut up by a Jo
or is it W.C.?
slant eye to slant eye talking
smooth talking or trying
"hey, baby _
looking nice tonight"
spilling sunrises
margaritas
bourbons with cherries
giddy easy striding to make it to my table
in your own eyes, a ghetto knight,
"wanna drink?"
in a flash and a flick, light my cigarette.
the dance floor is dead tonight
linoleum cracked
the Filipino D.J. Berkeley Asian American Studies dropout is stoned
and even the lights look neon sleazy
you want me to move, a wax museum dancing doll, under your
macho gaze
or in your arms, rocking following your rocks,
layered black hair
mustache, always, to tickle the quick kisses,
a cheap shiny shirt, four buttons open,
a jade pendant swaying against yellow brown flesh,
you want to take me home
and the grip on my shoulder tightens,
you driving a Camaro Z28?
an Olds 442?
a broken down Malibu?

a Caddy Eldorado?
you want to be rich someday
you want to enjoy life, you say,
'cuz it's so so short,
ALL girls want you for their old man
"in bed, I have a good body,
opium makes me last
and last
I'm ten inches
and," a smile,
"this thick."
you play the mind games with a too ridiculous seriousness
not another escape out just for kicks
your street male pride can take no scratches
you'll kick my ass when the number I give you isn't mine
you tell me not to dance with anyone else
when I just met you tonight
and isn't your old lady waiting at your apartment?
hardened hard up
rickshaw stray tiger cat
your life view
doesn't quite
touch mine
and being gangbanged isn't my type of thrill
disco steps don't silence sirens
and the skyscraper lights don't touch Grant Avenue
on a Friday night
Golden Dragon massacred meat can't ever be pieced back together
again
black lights and hanging ferns or Remy sweetness can't hide
spilled out alley fish guts
that tell you and tell you
there just
is no future
your hands grope
your eyes closed
your tongue dry
your penis limp
poor ChinaMAN-child

Cecil Taylor

Cecil Taylor's fingers are genius crazed mice, appearing and disappearing, light speed flashes of moments. *Cecil* himself, his shirted back, trickling sweat, then soaked wet, is a giant uncaged animal, arching, crouching, sometimes lovingly, but most of the time viciously, from the right side of the grand piano, where crystal clear sparkles of notes are triangularly cornered stars falling upon keyboards, all the way to the left hand side, groaning heavily with the growls emanating from the dark piano, now breathing so deeply with life. His unpredictable colors unbelievable originate from a hidden almost perverse yet ultimate, space of soul, outside any reality. That penetrate, fill your wholeness, that has already forgotten to resist. Concentrated muscle tense that is relaxing, freeing in the numbed hypnosis of his drugging power. Drinks lie untouched on the night club tables. Ears become one. And all other music, all other sound, all other thought can suicidally stop in shame before *Cecil*. When he rests, and he doesn't rest, he releases you to sigh in lyrics of relief, the beauty of jazz rhythms, only to thrust you back into the irregularly regulated chords he hears. Till you hear his hands, parting seas, red and black, back and forth. The mad jerkings of perpetual tears choked confusion in your chest are muted in an overwhelmed one-ness of peace. You are tiny, fantasy-filled, merely deformity caught in the immature evolutionary stages, but you are ecstatic to have stayed alive long enough to experience what you just experienced.
So that the world is no longer a void. But an eternal feeling blanketing cities, skies, machines and men.

Assumptions

when people bad-mouth us
sneering in French
assumptions are being made of us
a yellow face is non-literati,
good at math, grunts only pidgin
assumptions are being made of us
we are followers, never leaders,
happy to be hired
assumptions are being made of us
sidekick in "Heroes," never the hero
Kato like Tonto
assumptions are being made of us
we do dishes
we do blow-jobs
assumptions are being made of us
trying hard to be liked, blend in,
do better than the best
assumptions are being made of us
digging with a scalpel
make our slant eyes round
assumptions are being made of us
sneaky and un-scrup-u-lous
prove our loyalty by "going for broke"
assumptions are being made of us

Being Japanese: Kakijun, Enryo and Iki

KAKIJUN is something that could have significance only in Japan.

Kakijun refers to the rules on properly writing kanji characters _ specifically the order in which each stroke (traditionally rendered in paintbrush sumi-ink) must be written.

If you mess up the order, then it's wrong _ even if it looks exactly the same as if it had been written in the correct order.

Kakijun highlights the essential importance of process _ as opposed to results.

If it's not done the right way, it's wrong.

Japanese society emphasizes the Zen-like spiritual _ the virtue of what is happening within the individual _ form defining act _ not just Western-style pragmatism of getting things done, making money, winning status.

In another sense, kakijun is about fixating on regulations for the sake of appearances, not the substance of the action.

It penalizes deviations.

It discourages creativity.

It rewards conformity.

Still, kakijun can be a beautiful concept.

No wonder calligraphy looks a lot like abstract Western art.

It is forceful.

It is evidence of how the artist's individuality is expressed in form.

It is evidence of how Japanese art is defined as the beauty of the process.

Japanese rules of behavior _ how to enter a door, how to bow, how to drink tea _ are like Dance.

How you do something _ even everyday things _ is part of the definition of that person's value as a human being to all Japanese.

Pretty deep.

ENRYO is another super-Japanese concept.

Taken the bad way (let's start with that first this time), it's phony because it means: yup, you really want that second serving of cake but you don't want to look greedy so you act like you don't want it and say no, thanks, all the while hoping the host will realize you're just saying that and deep inside you want the cake and so will offer it again, no no no I insist, at which point you get to "give in" and eat the cake without feeling like a pig.

This is enryo.

And it's an everyday practice in Japan, even today.

This works only if the other party knows you are doing enryo.

It has been known to happen that if the other party for whatever reason fails to catch on and goes along with the preliminary refusal a la enryo-style, and doesn't persist in offering the cake, the originator of enryo can get quite resentful _ about not getting that cake after all _ and accuse the other person of all kinds of inadequacies, including not being a proper Japanese _ so delicate is this give-and-take interaction of enryo.

Enryo assumes that everyone is in the know.

Enryo evolved out of an insular small-village mindset.

But enryo is also soulful _ caring about the other person so much you're giving that person the chance to take his or her offer back, in case that person can't really afford to offer you that extra piece of cake.

Enryo is about self-sacrifice.

Enryo is about modesty.

It's about not being a totally egotistical and everyone-out-for-their-own kind of society.

It's about quiet graceful self-demeaning appearances taking precedence over who gets what and big egos and individualism.

Many other cultures besides Japan actually have enryo.

Americans may be a minority in not being hip to enryo at all, and in assuming that no one will be crazy enough to say No, to a desirable offer. Hey, why not? That's what a normal American would think.

And, well, why not?

If you have to ask, then forget about it.

That's what Enryo is.

IKI also sounds crazy
if you try to explain it to a hard-core pragmatist.
Iki means you do the most cool things where people can't possibly notice.
That's what makes it totally cool.
It's adoration of the less obvious, all the while hoping that the hidden wonders will somehow accidentally be noticed, making them even more superlative like a secret gift.
One good example of iki is a plain dark coat, the impeccable statement of understatement, which has as lining this ostentatious and intricate fabric.
The outer may be indigo but the innards would be an elaborate red and gold Hokusai-like manga design.
This is no joke,
and some Edo Period haori coats are just like that.
Or a kimono would be subdued but have this special lining at the collar that's only showing a tiny, tiny bit.
It defies logic, and that's why it's so iki.
The goal of a labor-intensive item is not to show off.
It's in and of itself precious _ although the argument can be made that iki is showing off of the ultimate,
perhaps most perverse, kind.
Even among Japanese, iki is supposed to be localized _ very Tokyo _ and some say down-home Osaka people don't value iki.
Iki means you never ask how much something costs.
Iki people would mix-and-match expensive items with weeds picked up off the road _ that kind of thing.
Like kakijun and enryo, iki is at once perception-oriented and arbitrary.
It's all about what people think but so specific it doesn't make any sense when you stop to think about it.
For those who swear by it, there are no gray areas.
And it is a good way to separate true Japanese from posers.

Dear Sir

Dear Sir,
do you love my daughter?
really love my daughter?
yes the one with the violin
holes in her jeans
she doesn't know she doesn't need you
just knows she wants
maybe the warmth of that moving
wormlike fetus stirring growing within her
maybe the hotness of those orgasmic waves
coming and going and coming within her
maybe that wet loneliness of wanting you and
wanting you when you aren't even gone
she sees only you
but do you love my daughter?
really love my daughter?
yes the one selling matches
begging at the train station
she needs to find herself
not end up being
maybe just one of your many conquests,
that pretty thing to have at your side
maybe that soul-mate you're keeping
while you're feeling too guilty to dump her
maybe that convenience
for cooking, counseling, coming that you don't even need
she will die for you
but do you love my daughter?
really love my daughter?
yes that search for love
of that woman for that man
it never ends, repeating
again and again

maybe that blood trickling painless
between our thighs on the abortion table
maybe that joy of a bouquet you bring
smelling of grease from the construction site
maybe that other woman you hide
like a fetish priest wishing my daughter's death
she isn't afraid
but do you love my daughter?
really love my daughter?

Strings/Himo

orphaned
i am your child
hunger of desperation
gnawing
my brain shrinks timidly
as i sit
a Japanese ghost at the bottom of a well
trapped in the dark
waiting
waiting
waiting
for you

only
once upon a time
time was endless

i dread your touch
when you return
that melts the hurt and vengeance
of wishing
to strangle you
with your umbilical cord that
still remains
dangling
rotten smelling
a lengthy piece of dried out squid

the nymph goddess beckons from a
sung dynasty painting
plump white cheeks
porcelain fingers
streaming black hair

Ikiru

When you cut your finger against the end of a piece of paper, and it hurts and the blood spurts out, you remember blood, lots of it, curdling red ink with a sweaty smell, is rushing around your body, all of it, brain, eyeballs, cell tissue, spine, toes, your heart is pumping like quivering red rubber and your lungs are going in and out, in and out.

When you stop to think about it, you want to scream and you almost forget how to breathe.

People who believe in reincarnation say it would be a waste of lives to have so many people alive and then die and so god must recycle all those lives.

It is nothing short of a miracle we continue to live every day despite all the deaths every day. And each one of us is dying gradually every day.

But for the most part, we don't get shot, we don't get run over, we don't crash, we don't get a deadly disease, we don't get stabbed, beaten to death, crushed in an earthquake, commit suicide, and we live live live live.

And each day adds to the next day and pretty soon we are old but still we live and we don't think about the blood circulating or the each and every breath we take or the fact that we have averted death for the moment.

We are alive.

But we could at any moment take a long silver needle and poke it in our eye, blinding ourselves in blinding rage.

We could jump into the wind from the station platform as the train glides in with a rattle, although the mirror is there to remind us how ghostly we look and make us think again how foolish this act is that we are contemplating to die this moment instead of the next moment when we do get shot or get cancer or our hearts stop or our lungs fail.

My mother is dying of pancreatic cancer, and I can finally smell death, that unmistakable stench that sticks inside your nostrils for hours, maybe even a day, trailing you from the hospice room. She has lost so much weight she looks like a bird, her nose pointed like a beak in a mummified face.

She lies curled up in the bed, her arms clasped into herself, a scrawny embryonic chick in a nest, and her beady eyes are expressionless, unmoving, staring into your eyes, and she won't close them because she knows you are her daughter and these may be the last moments, and she needs to look, but you just want her to close her eyes so you can leave and forget.

She couldn't even speak then.

When she could still move, when she was at the hospital, not the hospice, where patients are getting treatment to live, she was just a burden on the nurses and they wanted her to move to a hospice, she would grow delirious on pain-killers and start walking around the hallways naked, announcing: "I must leave now because Otoosama (her husband, my father) has arrived to get me."

My father is dead.

Before that, when she was still undergoing tests, and she had always instructed us she never wanted to know it, if she ever got cancer, and so we couldn't tell her, she says to me: "I wasn't a very good mother, was I?"

This is a very important conversation.

But I brush it off. I don't want to talk about this, do I? Because then wouldn't we be talking about her death?

"I watch you and your sister, how the both of you think about and interact with your children," she says. "And I realize I wasn't a good parent. I know this watching the both of you as parents."

She goes on, matter of fact, her father, who was a big believer in education and sent all his children, even the daughters, unusual for those times in Japan, to urban schools.

My mother was second from the youngest so she was barely in elementary school when she was sent to live away from home with her sisters and brothers to go to school.

And so she grew up never knowing the intimacy of a relationship between a mother and child.

She doesn't have to apologize. And I should reach out and hug her, but all I remember is how she never stopped him, her husband, my father, when he beat me, how I had to cower, never apologizing, and all she did was sit quietly and pray and be patient and believe the anger would pass like a typhoon, leaving behind just tiny purple bruise marks on sallow skin, as sanity returned to the Ph. D. in engineering, professor, salaryman, head of the household, and all would be well.

He needs a break from work, it is stressful, he needs to go to the family beach villa.

She has already made arrangements, and I must go with him, the ever faithful daughter because he can't go alone.

"It can't be me. It must be you," she says, as though this is decided, ironing the white shirts and folding them on top of each other on the tatami mat.

She doesn't tell me until later. She worried about me every day, praying he wasn't beating me.

He didn't beat me. We took turns rowing a wooden boat. We went fishing till our fingers smelled like worms. We lowered cages into the water with fish heads, and drew them up to find crabs entangled with each other.

But I can't forgive, not just yet, though no one has to apologize.

I call my sister on the train back from the hospital.

"She is going to die," I say, breathless, more from excitement than from sadness.

She is dying but she is realizing and she is changing.

What she is saying is so profound she had to be dying. Really dying.

It should have been like the movies.

I should have forgiven her, a moment of reconciliation before the moment of death.

You are a good mother.

Remember all the Ryunosuke Akutagawa stories you read to me in the kitchen, but you told me the stories I wrote, secretly, in big block letters in a worn out notebook were petty and would never amount to anything?

Remember how you wanted to go back to school for your Master's degree, but you had to cook and clean and you gave up?

Remember how you won awards with those elaborate sumi calligraphy on rice paper, painting ancient words no one could read?

Remember how you sat naked in the bath tub, thinking your solitary thoughts, and you hated your husband, my father, because he bought you the wrong-size ring in an overseas business trip?

Today, you taught me how people keep evolving till the last moment of life.

No, you are not a bad mother at all.

This is the best gift you have given me.

I have learned the lesson of death although I still can't understand how we manage to keep living day by day, lungs breathing and heart beating and you feel so far away and I can't remember anything else about you.

Music Land

I live with this strange animal of a man called "a musician." An obscure musician at that.

A typical day may start around noon. Or later. Always with music.

"I had this dream," he says in a weary tone, his consciousness still a half step within his subconscious. "I was about to outplay Kenji on stage. I was just getting to my solo when I woke up."

"Kenji, your own cousin?" My voice is muffled from under the sheets.

"Kenji's always laying all this shit on me. I'm basically a humble kind of person, but I think he has rhythm problems, you know."

I feel his body stretching toward the record player by our heads. I turn to his profile. Lying on his stomach, propping one palm against a cheek, he places the needle carefully. His eyes are almost closed, through the smoke of a stub he has picked up and lit from an over-filled ashtray that used to be a mayonnaise jar lid. The stub protrudes from the corner of his mouth, where the lips meet. The wispy smoke obeys its own lazy sense of rhythm as it wanders upward, drawing smoke signal curls in the air.

The window behind the blinds shows a small portion of the sky already taking on a grayish hue.

"No wonder Asian American music is, as you say, lame on all fronts," I remark.

He is not listening for his ears are busy absorbing the music from the record. He has sat up in his usual position, recalling an ape or a Neanderthal, his knee caps drawn close to his chest. He is nodding his head in time to the music. "Mmmm _ that's bad."

He picks up the needle in the middle of the tune to hear a certain section again. After about ten seconds, he replaces the needle to the same spot, muttering how the piano player is perfectly a shade off time, listens, again brings back the needle.

By the time he is ready to do this another additional time to the time I think is going to be the last time, I am getting out of bed. He grabs my waist, pulling me down, and nudges his body on top of mine. "Let's fuck."

Without waiting for an answer, he covers my mouth with his and begins squeezing my breasts, molding their fresh rice-cake softness till the nipples become two hardened erect points emerging from a whiteness pushed lopsided by his hands. He sucks like a famished baby on one nipple then quickly moves his tongue to the other, until a wetness, with a pleasure that is like pain, ekes out of my vagina.

He pushes my legs apart with his and fingers his penis inside me.

We call it "post-fuck euphoria," P-F-E for short. Meaning that I am so overwhelmed by his sexual powers that, at that moment, he can ask for anything, and I will give it to him. He takes everything I say, while in this state _ like "You have the greatest penis in the world," or "I'll kill you if you fuck with anyone else," with a grain of salt.

That is, everything I say that is coherent, which is after the fullest intensity of P-F-E has worn out, to a slow coming down, a falling from an Icarus dream flight, when you are soaring easily, without flapping your arms. With that weird sense of weightlessness, or, rather, of weight getting focused at the bottom of all your bones, when you lose all perspective of what is up or down, left or right, so that you are a disoriented and floating tiny spot of darkness within a darker universe, infinite in all directions.

Often he makes fun of this P-F-E phenomenon, arching his back on the bed, mimicking my gasps for breath, my moans and habit of biting my hand. But if I gain my articulation too soon after his great performance, he doesn't like that either.

I have never figured out if men are capable of the sensitivities involved in a P-F-E experience _ the relaxed, Zen-like acceptance of all things as they are. Expressed bluntly and simply without lofty pretentions: after I get fucked real good, long and hard, the world can go fuck itself.

He is being cool, sitting up in his characteristic position, puffing a cigarette. He usually listens to Miles Davis or John Coltrane, if it is late at night. Or he puts on whatever piece he has been practicing lately _ be it classical, rock or funk _ and plugs cords into his player and guitar. Sitting up naked on the bed, with earphones covering his head, and cuddling the cold curvatures of an electric guitar with his overly developed sinewy and vein-popping forearm, he resembles an alien space creature or else a mutated enlarged Kafkaesque insect of some sort.

If he is in a generous mood, you may get to play the privileged role of audience for a while, as he plays, wrinkling his nose and opening his mouth in a silent wail, in what he imagines is the seductively playful manner of a groupie-trailing rock star.

But, most likely, he will be lost to all reality. His long lashes will be blinking, dream-state rapid eye movements. A flush will spread on his neck and chest, but especially at the ears. A perverse strain of blood will be stirring within his veins _ the kind probably pulsating within miracle workers and mass murderers.

The band of cloth and leather, attached to the guitar, will bite gently into his back muscles, designed with rows of ribs, glistening with a thin coating of sweat. As though he is some athlete, working out, his shoulders will be pumped up with strangulated tension, as he stoops his head low over the instrument.

He is always physically close to me. But he is not really there.

Perhaps picking up after a man is a wifely duty.

I collect curled up socks that he has thrown on the floor. Browned apple cores covered with crawling ants. Cigarette stubs and used matches from knocked over ashtrays. And thin silver metal, broken off guitar strings.

We eat toast because there is nothing else to eat in the house.

Instead the house has a Filipino poet and a half-Filipino half-Japanese folk musician downstairs. Upstairs with us is a Caucasian homosexual, who is into growing mushrooms. Like some mad scientist, he has built a cardboard box with two holes for plastic gloves. He sprays Lysol into this construction with a care deserving of a vacuum tube.

A Chinese American acupuncturist also resides here. She is into spirituality and playing the chi'in. When I complained about a ghost sharing my first-floor room _ female, white, very old and very lonely (she wants me to read to her) _ she quietly instructed me not to pay attention to her; she's not even real and has the nerve to play upon my sympathies; and she burned herbs from Mexico, which filled the darkness of the room with their pungent odor. She swayed the smoking twig before her face.

Mice also live in this house. An argument could be made that it is the respect for life that prevents the extermination of the scurrying pests, but, since unsuccessful traps, with creative ideas, ranging from peanut butter to Chinese fermented bean curd, for bait, have been laid, the more likely reason is plain laziness or the tendency for a quick acceptance of all defeats in life. After all, transcendental adaptation is less painful than futile struggle.

"When are we going to move out of this house?" I ask him through a paper thin but nevertheless effective wall of the Sports pages that he has erected as he munches on whole wheat toast.

It is about two minutes later that he decides that I have spoken. When I grudgingly repeat the question, exaggerating the robotomized monotone in my voice, he smiles and reminds me that he's found a job _ driving Japanese tourists around the city of San Francisco in a van _ and goddammit, can't you stop bitching?

"Don't you ever want to be by ourselves? Just the two of us?" I ask with as much sweetness as a semi-liberated woman is capable of, thus trying not to sound bitchy.

"Of course, I do, baby." He goes back to the NBA playoffs.

"You know, I'm not getting any younger. I want to settle down, have a family." I pause. I try to get his attention with, "I want your baby," and, failing, tug at his wrist. "How come you never interact with me except through sex? Am I boring to talk to?"

He puts down the paper (he has already finished the toast) and draws me from my chair on to his lap. He kisses me and reassures me that he loves me; please be patient with him; I am the most important thing in his life _ "even more than music" _ this declaration calculated to surely melt my heart like a bar of butter in a desert.

Whereas, I don't see the meaning of the most beautiful music if the one that's creating it can't even make his loved ones happy. So what if he touches thousands of people? So what if he revolutionizes jazz? The man's fucked up.

I remind him I'm not about to play his Naima. Naima, by the way, was John Coltrane's first wife, apparently a member of the Nation of Islam and responsible, along with McCoy Tyner, for saving Coltrane from his alcoholism, drug addiction and other vices. In fact, for saving his life. So if it weren't for Naima, there would have been no "Love Supreme" or "Ascension" or any of that because there would've been no John Coltrane.

Naima and Coltrane separated, and he eventually married Alice, the pianist. After all, it makes sense _ if you're playing music practically every waking hour of the day, might as well marry a musician, too.

Poor Naima. I used to listen to the tune, "Naima" a lot, wondering what it was like to end up a neglected wife in real life and a tune that millions listen to, after or above life so-to-speak.

That the greatest musicians were assholes had occurred to me before, but it never intimately hit me, until a drummer insisted on fulfilling his performance commitment on the same night his woman was having a miscarriage. Since then, the image of my lover playing on some dirty stage _ his fingers acrobatically caressing the guitar neck, his pick holding strumming hand turned a pale blur within red-blue-yellow gel spots _ while I'm bleeding into sterilized hospital sheets, has been periodically creeping into my mind.

As a tangent note, this same drummer ended up escaping all the way to Japan, supposedly to study taiko drumming, but, also in the act, conveniently leaving the woman. Despite her efforts in joining a Japanese court-music troupe and taking up taiko, aside from the housecleaning, cooking and other domestic chores of love.

Women seem to have the habit of acquiring their men's interests, a confused distinction between wanting the interest _ music in the above case _ and wanting the man. I have known women who signed up for tennis lessons, who spent a small fortune on backpacking equipment, and one who went to the extent of experimenting in bisexuality, all in the name of sharing the man's interests.

The day I purchase a guitar is the day I die.

"If I ever want to become a good guitar player," he would say, his serious eyes looking directly into mine. "I have to practice."

He would sigh hopelessly. "Then you'd feel abandoned and unloved."

All this, after his proclamation that I am the only thing he has, the thing he loves more than music. And he keeps studying his fingers to check on how his calluses are faring.

To move out of the crazy house, to buy new instruments and an amplifier, to save money to go to New York, (almost forgot: to buy me an IBM typewriter and to make up for all the money I've put out for our past living expenses) _ for all these honorable causes _ he starts to work. And I mean, work, since this is a man of extreme extremes.

He gets up at six in the morning, takes a shower, gets dressed, dons a borrowed tie, and, with a hurried kiss to me, still in bed, he is gone, until ten or eleven at night because Japanese tourists want to go out for dinner, for drinks, to a star-lit, city-lit viewpoint, etc., etc.

So I am abandoned anyway.

When he comes home, he has about three hours or less of consciousness left. He is a tired body of a man, and I have no husband. I ask him to decrease his hours, maybe take a day off.

"Why can't you understand?" he says in frustration. He is especially tired and frustrated because he has had a couple of drinks with the other drivers on the way home.

"I was waiting for you all day. I cooked dinner. Though our housemates probably ate it all, by now."

"I wanted to get fucked up. They came down on me at the office today for being late."

Stifling an irreverent chuckle for his suburbanite phrase, "at the office," I nag again, "Why can't you get drunk at home? Why do you have to be like those Japanese company men? Our ancestors didn't immigrate here to have to deal with that bullshit."

"The drivers, they all hate the company." He starts to take off his clothes. "I have to go at least one more time, though, 'cuz they bought my drinks." I note that his entire body has turned red from Chivas Regal.

"Why didn't you pay for your own drinks? Fuck that Asian obligation shit."

"I'd feel bad. Are you jealous?" He climbs on the bed, lies on his back, with a sigh of exhaustion, and pulls the covers up to his chin.

I am still sitting on the bed, maintaining a stern expression.

"I'm so tired," he mumbles. "I have to work tomorrow."

"You promised last night that you'd take tomorrow off." I bang the phone on the bed. "Call them right now and tell them."

Still lying on the bed, he dials the phone, fumbling for the holes like a blind man. As soon as there is an answer on the other end, however, he has half-risen, scribbling with a pen the instructions for the following day's route. I shut the phone off with my finger. He dials again, apologizing for being cut off, and proceeds to finish receiving orders. I throw his jacket at him. He keeps talking.

After he hangs up, he tries to hold me. "Come on," he says.

I jump off the bed and slap his inviting arms away. "You promised." I hear myself sounding infantile.

"I didn't promise a thing. It's only for a few more weeks. Until I make some money. Isn't our love strong enough to last four weeks?"

"But what happened to workers' rights? Why do you have to kiss their ass? Okay _ I'll call them. What's their number?"

Having lain back on the bed, he is laughing with a sheer helplessness, shaking his head in disbelief. I leave him in his incredulity, look up the number myself, call the company and ask for the manager. I feel like screaming I want my husband back. Instead, I tell him in Japanese that my husband has a concert tomorrow night; he cannot, absolutely cannot, work tomorrow, no, not even for the morning only; he hasn't slept all week; his having to work from morning till night; you can go ahead and fire him, if you wish. The man on the line sounds a little bewildered but polite.

"You got the day off tomorrow," I announce.

"You make me look like a fool. I'm a pussy-whipped spineless jellyfish." Having admitted this insightful revelation to himself, he decides he doesn't like it. He is going to call up "the office" and tell them he will work tomorrow. I disconnect the phone. He re-connects it. I disconnect it again, at which point, in a foreboding display of his superior physical strength, he yanks the phone from me.

I have to remind myself that history has demonstrated that this man, in an intoxicated state, has a volatile potential for the most psychotic and sadistic of behavior. I turn to coaxing him. "He says you have the day off. See? He understands, if you tell him."

He gives up and replaces the receiver. He returns to bed. "Goddammit _ you're driving me crazy. You bitch about wanting to move out, and here I am, working my ass off for you. I can't do anything right by you. And I'm not going to be working there for the rest of my life _ even for you."

I don't feel particularly sorry for him, but I lie next to him and place my cheek on his naked chest. "I want you. I need you," I whisper into his mouth, my lips touching his. "I'm not asking for all that much; am I? I want you to be with me _ sometimes."

"Can't you see? I'm flat broke." He is yelling now. "All I have to my name, right now, is about thirty dollars in tips. And it's been that way since _ God knows when. We need money now. We set some goals, don't you remember?"

"But the reason I want to move out is because I love you." I switch strategies to appeal to logic. "In the means of achieving the ends, you're fucking up the ends. If there's no relationship, what's the use of getting our own place? Or having the prettiest guitars? You're so soulless and mechanical." I realize that I am being mean, so I lighten up. "If we can't move out, I'll learn to live with it."

"Bullshit!"

"We'll always have to work to pay rent."

"I don't need you to tell me that."

"We can't make long-term plans. It's going to be hand to mouth, hand to mouth, for the rest of our lives." Deep inside, I'm wishing I had married a doctor.

Perhaps, reading my thoughts, "Why don't you go back to your ex? He made money."

"Do you want me to?"

"It's up to you."

"It's up to *you*."

"No, it's up to you."

I snuggle closer to him. "Do you want to get rid of me?"

"Un—nuh." He shakes his head. He mutters to the ceiling, "I love you." Then, turning toward me, "What if we go on welfare and move into the slums? I used to know a guitar player who did that? Would you be able to stand it?"

I feel a sight sickness in my stomach. I want to tell him to quit romanticizing the impoverished musician life.

"I know where you're coming from," he is saying. "You don't understand me, though. Right now, I'm not making any money; I'm not taking care of you; I'm not even playing music. You don't care if I play music or not; do you? It's unethical to make people believe I'm a musician when I don't even play." He pauses dramatically. "I don't feel like a man."

I feel nervous, sensing the Third World emasculation syndrome coming on. "What do you want me to do?" He is silent. "If you are better off without me, since you can't take care of my needs and prove your macho-hood at the same time, that's that."

Suddenly, he sits up on the bed. "Why can't you understand what I'm going through?" he wails. "Why can't you understand?" He grabs my T-shirt, till I hear stitches tearing, and the collar rubs, almost chokingly, against my neck. "Get out of this house! I hate your guts. You'll never find a man that'll make you happy. You'll be searching forever."

Too late, I realize that his psychosis has attacked. He throws me down on the bed. Instinctively I cover my head. I start to cry. After pushing me around a few times, he calms down and lies back. "I'm so confused. I'm going insane. I've lost all perspective. I don't want you to go." He whispers the last line. His face is strained into a wince.

This time, I genuinely feel sorry for him and stroke away his tears, that are singular drops, falling slowly from his closed eyes, against his flushed skin, into his hair, making it damp. I kiss his face lightly in many spots. "You're tired. Do you want something to eat?" He shakes his head. "Do you want an orange?" He nods.

He sniffles a little as he peels the orange.

Music fills the dark hall.

The college used to be a mortuary, and I sense the ears of past ghosts turning to these sounds. The saxophone screeching with a morbidity of an extinct reptilian bird. The guitar crying, each note of the scales, falling tears turning mid-air into electrified pear-shaped crystal.

His eyes shut, his body bent, he has the same expression he has when he makes love. He plays with the same demonic insistence, the same urgent energy, as though he is aware of a secret danger that this moment now may be the last. And I know that I love him. That I have never loved anyone as I love him.

The music penetrates. Not only through the eardrums but also through opened goose-skin pores. Through liquid vibrations in the blood risen close to the surface, traveling to the heart. To all the organs, like a drug shooting through veins, like the slow but sure healing of swallowed herbs.

The reed player glances toward the second row, where his wife is sitting next to me. He quickly faces downward.

My hands are wet. I place them under my thighs for fear I will start scratching myself.

Thinking is erased from my brain. There is no room, filled by his music _ amplified voices, the moans, shouts and laughter of music, that are almost visible like laser beam light waves before my eyes.

When they finish, I turn around. I find that the small crowd which had been seated in the hall previously has filtered out during their set. There is only one other man, clapping politely. He appears slightly embarrassed.

The musicians are crouched over, enclosing their instruments into their cases. I study his expressionless face. He looks almost bored.

I go up to him and slip my arm around his, leaning into his shoulder. And, as he returns a feeble smile, I tell him, softly, into his ear, "Thank you."

Caution: Coast and Surf Area
extremely dangerous
People were Swept
and have drowned

each chrysanthemum
her lover's soul
she arranges/ clipping
pushing into golden needles
   sunk beneath the celadon lake
as furin bells to the summer wind
stir straw scents about her tabi feet
gently folded, toes over toes,
digging the sabi tones
of her zabuton
her eyes mirror
the proud triad
one stooping, petal barely glancing
wild leaved violets covering the stems

I am an artist

I give of myself

a midnight geisha
she combs her wet
konbu hair by the cemetery
singing
without lyrics
or melody
or rhythm
the basic blues on the shamisen

she squats
lighting the honeyed red oil of
the akari
waiting for her lover
she is the crazed picture-bride
scrubbing hardened maggot rice
in daidokoro darkness
running through wheat fields
lopsided
toward the dots of stars
her bare feet bleeding through blisters
her heart storming between wire hanger shoulders
her hair a mane around
waif eyes, expressionless,
    focusing nothing
    seeing everything
she wipes her nose
then keep on waving
till her fingers dried
are invisible bird wings
flapping from her wrist

I am a writer
who sees unreality in reality
walking the spider web line
that snaps,
dissolves,
milkened eyeball con-caved
like peeling plaster that
mice movements
crumple off ceilings
I am the bell jar
that breaks
a thousand pieces
till all space
in-between

all sky
all silences between words
fall
becoming one
stifling, drowning, dying
with the dawn
into life _
spreading in all directions
outward and
inward _
molecular
(buzzing in each grain of my man's air)
solar systems of
eternal universe internal

the alien from the Realm of the Senses
the community J-town whore
she laughs through false eyelashes
a half-broken Noh mask
at the Kabuki bar
she's the Wah-Ching girl
who fucks a Jo
though her uterus emptied is
silk-woven with scars
she never rests
doing "the dog"
draped in sequins at Eppamanados

I am
open
a bottomless well
within earth
swallowing earth

I will not cry, except in love.

People Who Know Pain

The World is divided
Between two kinds of People
The Winners and the Losers
The Takers and the Givers
The Famous and the Forgotten
The Loved and the Unloved _
Those who don't care and

People who know Pain
People who know Pain

when your tongue rolls, the
tips of my nipples, piercing
knife of betrayal

Vincent Van Gogh
John Coltrane
Garcia Marquez
Toulouse Lautrec
Billie Holliday
Richard Wright
Kenji Miyazawa

People who know Pain
People who know Pain

baby foxes dance,
leaving paw marks in the snow,
fairy tale of joy

Hermit, victim,
Outcast, untouched,

Untouchable
They travel faceless
Shadows on the subway
Mute, unconnected,
Unknowing of their own Pain

People who know Pain
People who know Pain

bitter memories grow
a cancer pomegranate
bleeding and rotting

I'd rather shelter that Pain alone
A powerless nobody,
Ashamed, shunned,
Stench of insignificance,
Laughing the idiot's laugh,
Running forgotten errands,
Dying before living like other

People who know Pain
People who know Pain

a zillion light years
the planet pulsates timeless
soundless universe

I'd never be that superior someone who
Conquers, fornicates, lynches,
Deposits paychecks, plans careers,
Forms opinions, writes reviews,
Weighs pros and cons, wins awards,
Attends receptions, discriminates,
Never knowing, shrugging off, how Painful

People's Pain can be
People's Pain can be

Story of Miu

(1)

Miu, 16, likes living in Tokyo because as a Japanese American she never felt she fit in her surroundings quite as well when she was growing up in the Washington D.C. suburbs, the only Asian in her class, although there were a few other Asians in her school whom she avoided the best she could, so embarrassing was it to be reminded of how she looked, how she stuck out _ the straight black hair, the almond slant gook eyes, dark, not blue and airy like the others. And the pale yellow sallowness of her skin, almost a khaki tone, sand of the desert, dried fruit rinds, not translucent and crystalline like a Botticelli painting, like the others. Miu used to sit in the foggy mist of the bathroom, scrubbing her arms in the tub, hoping/praying to turn white. Here in Tokyo, her skin turns suddenly a normal color. It caught even herself by surprise. If she wears her Ne-net clothes, and sits crossing a frail booted leg on the sidewalk-railing of Harajuku, lazily watching the street peddlers and Costume-Play teen-agers, she knows she blends in. So perfectly. She doesn't even need to keep her mouth shut. She studied Japanese in high school so actually she can speak Japanese quite well, as long as she keeps her sentences short and simple. Boys even try to pick her up, as though she is any other Japanese girl waiting for such advances, sweet, ripe, pungent but colorless. Back in the U.S., the boys who bothered to desire her were those with a fetish for Asian women. It was sadly obvious. They were the ones with a string of Asian girlfriends, one after the other, and in her neighborhood that required some searching. When for whatever reason, they broke up, she'd find out they had hooked up with yet another Asian girl. Being Asian was a brand. A categorization you could never escape, especially in how you attracted the opposite sex. Dating Asians was out of the question, Miu says, because there were only two or three Asian males for miles around, and they were always fat or ugly, or had a white girlfriend. Miu made a point to come out to Tokyo just to get away.

(2)

More from Miu: What I remember about him is the smell of his breath, like candy gone sour, when he said, putting his lips close to my ear: "I found another girlfriend where I moved. She is Japanese. But I don't like her the way I like you." I was still in elementary school, and so I didn't quite analyze what it was about Asian women or about that boy that could be behind this penchant for the yellow race. He was too young to have seen old G.I. World War II movies, or looked up books on geisha or Suzy Wong. But I was the symbol of beauty for this person. He followed me home from school, offering me a bouquet of buttercups he'd picked from the lawn. He caught my arm and we tumbled together on the grass in simulated intercourse, male body on top of female body, his breath over my breath. Secretly I hated him. This tall lanky male of sweet-and-sour breath, Dennis the Menace, straw hair, pale freckles, blue of his eyes that seemed to connect to the sky above the buttercups _ the markings of the race that's so Dick and Spot, Hollywood, Marvel Comics, the evening news, rock 'n' roll. I told him to stay away. But he wouldn't stop as though he couldn't believe an Asian he had picked could possibly not like him. I was a target, a thing, not allowed to have thoughts on my own.

(3)

Recently Miu and I had dinner at an Indian restaurant in Shiodome, where Japanese belly-dancers came sashaying out (to the yelps of suit-clad salarymen sitting at another table) right in the middle of dessert.
Miu and I discussed sexual fetishes and how race comes into play although we weren't exactly sure what it meant.
"Pocahontas. Suzy Wong. Thomas Jefferson's slave," Miu said pensively.

"Nonwhite women are so used to feeling honored to be seen sexually desirable by the Opposite Sex at large but especially the white male."

The pasty stomachs of the dancers rolled around to the music as bells jangled and eyelashes fluttered.

"Does India even have belly-dancing?" she asked exasperated.

Miu tells me she has made an important decision.

"I am never going to open up my legs to another white male ever," she announced.

"Race should not matter, but we are all products of history, and what we do can't be taken out of context of what people did before us because that's what's going on in people's heads. I'm going to find me a boyfriend in Tokyo who is like Bruce Lee," Miu said.

First of all, Bruce Lee is from Hong Kong.

And I didn't even have the heart to tell her that Bruce Lee married a white woman, and supposedly wasn't 100 percent Asian himself. It is sad, though.

Miu told me there was a guy she dated back in the U.S. who explained to her matter of factly that he had discovered Asian women had softer skin than did other races _ as though that was supposed to be a compliment.

(4)

Japanese summers are never complete without Bon Odori, the neighborhood thanksgiving celebration of the harvest, the annual homecoming of ancestral ghosts, the end of summer.

The dress code: cotton yukata kimonos in white, indigo and goldfish red, splashed with bold patterns of flowers, bursting fireworks, waves of water. Wooden clogs or woven straw slippers on the feet. Big uchiwa fans, the kind that don't fold out gracefully, upper-class, but just stay flat (also with bold patterns) to get flapped around to swat mosquitoes and cool off in the evening breeze.

The smell in the air: Grilled noodles, pancakes and octopus dumplings topped with seaweed and dried fish, peddled at stalls set up like tents, which also sell manga-character masks, goldfish, shaved ice, bobbing balloon yo-yos, chocolate-covered bananas on sticks.

The sound: Deep intestine-curdling thumps of a taiko drum from a stage that's set up _ just for the weekend.

The drum plays in time to funky songs. Some are minyo folk tunes, but others are pop concoctions, like "Tokyo Ondo," which has become the rallying theme song for the Yakult Swallows, a Tokyo baseball team, and children's songs like "Anpanman" or "Obakyu Bon Odori."

The drummers play loud and strong.

They strike poses, fling their arms, twirling and throwing their sticks, staccato out rhythms, swinging with the beat.

The dancing goes in a circle around the stage, repetitions of steps, arm moves and turns that don't require acrobatic skills to execute (although the instructors on stage _ you can pick them out because they wear the same white and blue yukata _ do every move with a certain elegant nuance you can't imitate without taking real lessons.)

Maybe there are only five, six choreography patterns you have to get in your head, but each song is a little different and so it's harder than you think.

Most of the time you end up looking totally ridiculous.

Never mind _ the point isn't about showing off.

The point is about getting down and having fun and doing the best you can.

And knowing another summer is over.

"Oh, this is so much fun," said Miu, who had never been to a real Bon Odori before, wiping sweat she's worked up from dancing. "There is something about this place that's movie-like. It's surreal."

Something about those lanterns hung from the poles and around the makeshift stage bouncing in time with the embryonic heartbeat booms of the drum surround that place where we are gathered in a soft, strange glow _ reminding us of both our cosmic isolation and the terrible death that is so always there but telling us all this in a warm, comforting way, like a grandmother telling us a story: It's going to be okay; there is nothing to be afraid of.

The way I explained it to Miu is that when the moment comes for me to die, and flashes of images like a multicultural slide show play in my mind in a lazy dozing off of death, somehow, I know Bon Odori will be one of those scenes.

My son was just 6 when he played drums with the other children at his first Bon Odori. He was barely bigger than the drum, challenging the drum until blisters tore his fingers.
He is 25 this year.
It's not hard to understand why Japanese believe ancestral ghosts come home for Bon.

(5)

I got a letter from Miu:

Hi,
Just dropping a note to tell you about my first ever outing to Shinjuku's Nichome district.
I was out with a couple friends for midnight mugs of beer at a tiny dingy cafe bar that spilled out into the alleys, dotted by sex-toy shops and gay bars, lonely souls occupying their time between yesterday and tomorrow _ one of those rare places in ethnocentric Tokyo where status/national origin/even sexuality go out the window.
Or so you'd like to think.
Then suddenly this Japanese guy comes up to me: "Are you with somebody?"
His next question: "Are you looking for gaijin?"
That bar, like others in that scene and Roppongi, attracts a fair share of foreigners.
I'd never forget that look in his eyes _ so afraid, so pathetic, so sad.
It was a totally depressing end to the evening.
What happened to this nation with its supposed reputation for right-wing conservative stuck up glorification of Japanese-ness!?
It's like reliving colonialism.
You read about how Japanese women are staying single because they earn their own livelihood and don't find the marrying lifestyle particularly attractive.
But my question is: Do they find the Japanese male attractive?
It would be a total lie to deny this phenomenon _ hordes of Japanese women who thrive on relationships with foreigners, seek them out at bars, hang from their arms, a modern-day Madame

Butterfly, and worship the foreigner, even unattractive ones, for their foreign-ness!

There's a sexual crisis of some sort going on between the Japanese male and the Japanese female.

They don't find the physical traits, mannerisms, social connotations from their own peers erotically arousing.

They find the alien intriguing.

Maybe exoticism is sexy by definition. But isn't that just a fetish, and certainly not a way to a healthy romantic relationship?

Help!

Miu

My reply to Miu:

How can you blame the Japanese female for seeking Western-style liberalism in attitudes toward women?

And how can you blame the Japanese female for their definitions of sexual beauty and sexual relationships when they have been fed Hollywood from birth?

And how can you blame the Japanese female for seeking personal partners outside Japanese society, when so many are doing so already with their careers (practically forced to do so, given sexism at major Japanese companies)?

But I see your point.

It is unfortunate how their personal lives fit like a jigsaw puzzle into the larger oppressive landscape of race/sex/class.

When Black Power rose in the 1960s, part of that was an awakening by the people to face up to that to overcome those larger social forces in their personal lives _ by redefining beauty, sexuality, love.

But the problems of cooking for/sleeping with/kissing XXX for the Male Master simply don't get fixed by switching His Color.

Staying within one's Color certainly simplifies the dilemma by at least knocking off one possible horrible fetish one has to confront in a sexual relationship.

But that's about it.

Just curious, but what happened in the end with that Japanese guy in Nichome?

Stay well,

Yuri

(6)

Miu and I went to a disco called The Room in Shibuya.
And it was as tiny and shabby as a room.
People stood next to each other in rows and shifted their weight
from one leg to the other nervously to the thump-thump of music
as a mirror ball glistened sadly from a corner.
Miu says this is the new, tucked-away look of Tokyo discos.
The big slick ones with shiny floors are obsolete, although they
apparently still exist in parts of Roppongi, where old men, many
of them foreigners, try to pick up young Japanese women.
We were not dressed appropriately in our T-shirts and jeans.
You must wear short skirts and tops with your breasts about to
fall out, then people will want to talk to you and want to have sex
with you, according to Miu.
A disco is a place where boys take girls they pick up on the streets:
(1) By dancing, the male can make sexual overtures to the female
and find out her interest/ lack thereof in having sex.
(2) By dancing, the female will get tired, allowing the male to
suggest going to a hotel to have sex.
A disco delivers relatively high returns for low investment.
Dating for weeks to just kiss isn't efficient.
"There has to be someone out in the world who is your true love,"
Miu says, shouting a bit over the music.
"Romantic love must exist. Like Romeo and Juliet. Or is that
unreal like a father's ghost or a forest moving, which aren't at all
everyday like a disco?"
Miu says a man she got to know recently says he finds someone
like Juliet a bit too much.
I'll tell her maybe it's better to hang out with another Capulet, or
how about my friend Mercutio?
I may be someday someone's Romeo but I will never find a Juliet,
he told Miu.

(7)

Suddenly, strangely, Miu feels power turn on like a tungsten flame
inside her _ maybe that hot spot in between her breasts. And her
breath turns a bit quicker, warmer.

As a young Asian female, she never feels power anywhere else _ at high school, at shopping malls, at summer jobs, even at home, she has long grown used to her role that is not to challenge but to accept and approve.

But in that dingy darkness of that Tokyo club, she, and others like her, have truer deeper powers.

The heads turn, their eyes shiny like those of hungry animals in a cave sniffing for prey.

She knows all she has to do is return that look to have them do whatever she wants—get off their chairs in a scamper, rushing to her at her beck and call: "Hi, are you alone?" "What's your name?" "Do you want a drink?"

It is merely up to her whim to choose which of those young men will be that lucky one.

She doesn't want the easy ones. She doesn't want the obviously handsome ones.

Being so easy and so obvious, such a catch does not speak to the heights of her powers.

That's not the kind of entertainment she is looking for on this night out on the town with her girlfriends _ her shoulder-length hair neatly rolled like Cinderella's, her skinny legs showing flesh, stockingless, beneath her short patent-black boots, her clutch bag covered with Swarovski crystals.

The man must be worthy of all this work and investment and taste, she thinks, laughing to herself.

And the man, naturally, must have that undiscovered look.

Shy, quiet and impeccably innocent, downcast eyes hiding under soft bangs, he doesn't know how beautiful or how bestial he can be, until he meets her, she muses.

She doesn't have any specific characteristic in mind _ he doesn't have to be tall, dark, smart, rich _ he can be anything and everything as long as he has that something special that makes her feel powerful not only over him but over everyone else who has looked down upon her for being Asian, young and female and has forgotten to credit her with the intelligence, insight and passion of choosing how to live life.

He must look at her as his all in that moment when they exchange glances and he approaches her and they dance, moving their hips in time to that deafening beat, and he must believe, as she does, that they have known each other from the beginning of time.

Which one is that special man? She scans the scene, taking her time, going from one dirty room to another, balancing herself carefully on the spiral metallic staircase on golden stiletto heels. When she sees him, it can't be more definite or fatalistic.

She walks up to him, standing, looking bored, so undistinguished and so plain and so unknowing by the giant speakers blasting with noise, so one-way is this selection, hers and not his.

He may even be there, waiting for his girlfriend, or he is drinking away his disappointment because his girlfriend has chosen to go somewhere else, or luckier still, he has just broken up and isn't quite ready to look for someone new.

This is important: That she picks him, not the other way around. She reaches up to his neck, pulls his face down gently, as though she needs to whisper an urgent question.

He accommodates, not too eager, just because he is trying to be nice to someone who may have a question, and as he faces her, she puts her mouth to his, forcing her tongue through his cold lips, and their tongues merge as one in the best kept secret in that club, that night, that city, that universe.

Her mind goes blank. And all she sees is that soft black one-ness inside her head, swirling, and she feels happy as though the games people play and the question of who is powerful no longer matter.

(8)

(Scene: A Kyoto-style restaurant on the 14th Floor of the Takashimaya Department Store in Shinjuku, Tokyo. The delicately shaped servings in modern geometric cups and plates line a wooden counter facing wall-to-wall glass that overlooks a noontime luscious view of Shinjuku Gyoen garden.)

Miu (Fingering traditional "tenugui" cotton towels the restaurant has given as napkins): Cool!

Me (Trying not to sound too curious): And so how's it going?

Miu: Okay.

Me: You were telling me you picked up . . . met someone, right, the other day? And so what's the latest news?

(Silence for several minutes; waiter from the other side of the counter brings cups of tea.)

Miu: Yes, there have been developments. He said we were supposed to meet at Alta in Shinjuku _ that was, I guess, last weekend _ to see a movie. But I didn't go.

Me: You didn't go.

Miu (Shaking head): But I did meet another guy. I went to a different club with some other friends, and there was this other guy.

Me: That's great.

Miu: Actually, I am building a database.

Me: What?

Miu: I figure you have to be scientific about this procedure. (Begins to explain hurriedly) My Japanese really improves, spending time with these guys. Free lessons! (Laughs.)

Me: And so how does the database work?

Miu: It's easy. You collect phone numbers. It must be harder for males but for females, you don't have to do much.

Me: And how many have you collected?

Miu: Lots. I haven't checked.

Me: Like 10? 20?

Miu (Giggling): More like 100.

Me: Gosh. How can you possibly keep track?

Miu: That's the challenge. You have to take good notes _ oh, you'd know about that. How do you keep track of all the people you interview?

Me: I have to write down the person's characteristics on their meishi. Thank God Japanese are into their meishi.

Miu: What do you write?

Me: Like "did most of the talking," "said nothing," "glasses," "made joke about such and such." It's tough. They tend to be all male and old and wear dark suits.

Miu: Similar problem here. All male, young, eager to get into bed, very very boring!

But I write down what they said and stuff. And I can sometimes even take their photo with my cell phone. My cell phone has a better digital camera than my camera.

Me: At least, you are getting around and meeting a lot of people and learning about Japan. And no sense rushing into settling down with one person. Maybe I could have gotten someone better if I had held out, too. (Sighs)

Miu: Oh, don't say that. You have a great marriage.

Me: Thanks. So what do you do with all that information? You call one of them up randomly when you need to go out or something?

Miu: Something like that.

Me: Your generation _ there is so much technology available like SNS, e-mail, messaging, all that, to connect in so many ways maybe you don't feel like you've checked out all your options unless you build this . . . database. (Miu shrugs as we eat with lacquered chopsticks soy-flavored grilled fish, chopped seaweed and daikon in vinegar sauce and miso soup with tofu.) The world was a simpler place when all you did was sit around at home and wait for a call on that fixed line.

Miu: You didn't do that, did you?

Me: Of course, I did. Everybody did. What if he calls and you're out? You'd miss that chance to go out with him, right?

Miu: How could you stand it?

Me: Right, it was quite oppressive, wasn't it? (Pauses) Yes, you're right. The new technology is progress. But don't you feel that Japan is still stuck in the 1950s as far as images of women?

Miu: What do you mean?

Me: There aren't that many outlets for older women still, except maybe flamenco classes for housewives or something. We know studies say more women are working and some are even successful. We see them on TV. But the most desirable roles for women are defined as young and cute because it's the men who are behind the definitions. I mean, look at the U.S. presidential race. What a contrast.

Miu: But maybe Yuriko Koike will run for the LDP presidential race, and there you go: Japan's first female prime minister.

(Miu and Me laugh.)

Me: What comes to mind when you hear "obasan?" Nothing good, right?

Miu: No one wants to be called "obasan." That's like the worst derogatory thing in Japanese you can call a woman.

Me: There is "babaa."

(They laugh. Waiter brings dessert, a traditional rice-cake pastry with fruit and sweet black beans)

Have you noticed what word the sales people at Shibuya 109, the Kyoto "maiko" and night club hostesses use to refer to older women to avoid saying "obasan?"

Miu (Visibly curious): No, what?

(They sip tea.)

Me: "Oneesan."

Miu: Oneesan.

Me: Forever young _ although older. But I think this shows how society hasn't recognized the value of the female after women have gotten past their roles of reproduction.

Miu: Oh, wasn't there some minister who got in trouble for calling women "reproductive machines?"

Me: Exactly. That mentality. There are lots of women in their 30s and older who truly dread being called "obasan." If it hasn't happened already, then it could happen any second. Horrors!

Miu: Moment of metamorphosis. Society decrees you useless for preservation of the species.

Me: I like being obasan. I am proud of being obasan.

Miu: OK, obasan.

Me: Obasan is a title that you earn as a woman when you grow older and wiser and better. Sounds a bit like sour grapes, doesn't it? But I think I learned so much about womanhood _ maybe "personhood" _ through my motherhood _ or through my son, I guess, having a child.

Miu: That's wonderful.

Me: All the years my son was growing up, his friends who spoke Japanese would call me obasan. They would look at me with those big innocent eyes of theirs, trusting me because I was their friend's mother. It's respect I earned not only because of my relationship with my son but also my son's relationship with others. That's why I get to be obasan. It's real and very beautiful and full of dignity. Not some derogatory place in the hierarchy as defined by sexual desirability, work performance, whatever. It's deeper than all that.

Miu: It is. And it should be like that.

Me: Women should be proud of being obasan.

Miu: Of course.

Me: Obasan Power!

Miu: That's a good way to put it.

Me: But all you see in the Japanese media much of the time are obasans rushing to bargains, gossiping, taking flamenco lessons.

Miu: What's the solution?

Me: I'm not sure. Data show Japanese women are choosing not to get married and not to have children, even if they do by some miracle get married. (Looks into Miu's eyes.) I try to tell young women this every chance I get, but it's the most important experience in life to have a child, Okay? No one really told me this. I was so lucky I did get married and have a child. The common wisdom back then was that women had to prove we could be just as good as men. And so worrying too much about marriage and children was seen as backward, something that women who weren't "liberated" (Holds up her hands to make quotation marks in the air with her fingers) did _ not women who wanted to make something of themselves and have careers.

Miu: I want a child. Maybe not now. But I want a baby someday.

Me: You will. You will. And you have plenty of time. To build databases and everything else.

Miu: This database I am building isn't about that though. I'm not sure what it's about. But I don't want to be trapped by someone just because he picks me out from the crowd. Why do I have to wait for some coincidental accident in the office elevator or some freakish event like in a TV drama to meet someone?

Me: Maybe old-style Japan was on to something when they had omiai for an arranged marriage. That's pretty orderly. So Japanese.

Miu: Then I wouldn't have to spend all this time on a database.

Me: Someday you will meet that special person _ that man who will throw that whole database out the window.

Miu (Silent then): How do you know?

Me: You'll know. You won't have to ask.

Miu: I will hear my heart go thump thump. Uh-oh, I think that's just the music blasting off at the club. I probably won't be able to hear it _ it's so loud in there (Laughs).

(9)

The "plop plop plop" of electronic waterdrops sound from my cell phone, the ringtone I've set so I know it's e-mail from Miu.
On the subject column, an animation icon of a glittering pink heart bounces around.
"It's him!" her message reads, a little ominously.
I press the tiny keyboard quickly with my thumb for an immediate reply: "Who he?"
It turns out she recently joined a world-music band with African drums, guitar, keyboards, traps drumming and singing that she was introduced to by a friend in high school.
Miu is learning how to play the kpanlogo with this group.
But more importantly, she has met someone.
He is the band leader Yuga. He's 21, and so a few years older than Miu.
This is what Miu says, a bit breathless on the phone, when I call her in the evening after I get home from work:
He has the most beautiful dark eyes like those of a wise elephant.
He writes songs about being free, being in love and never forgetting the passion for life.
And what is fascinating about him is that he is not interested in money, status or careers, Miu says.
He works for a Tokyo dot.com that is contracted out to create ringtones for mobile phones.
And this is apparently a lucrative business because every tune on the Japanese pop charts has to be programmed into a ringtone.
But there's special software to do it so it's pretty easy, leaving Yuga a lot of time to work on his art, like composing, writing lyrics, collaborating with illustrators, rehearsing for performances and working on sound engineering on recordings.
Some of his songs are movie scores because the trend for some of the most mainstream Japanese movies lately is to use "indies" soundtracks.
As I gather from what Miu tells me, this person has never been abroad and doesn't understand any English.

He doesn't even have a passport, Miu says with a giggle, as though that only adds to his charm of being someone totally genuine whom only she has discovered.

He speaks with a slight accent of the Sea of Japan, which makes the speaker's tone softer than the Tokyo dialect, as though that person is somehow in perpetual doubt.

The shifts in intonation are similar to the speaking style of Korean actors that older Japanese women are so crazy about, like "Yon-sama," Miu says, to her, another profound observation.

Not that I like Yon-sama at all, Miu adds with a laugh.

He calls me "MEEEH-you-san," it sounds so sexy!

There isn't much point in contesting her observations.

I know Miu is in no mood to be challenged about any of them, anyway.

I am invited next weekend to what's called "raibu," short for "live performance," meaning a concert, where I will have an opportunity to meet Yuga.

But I am more happy for her than worried.

I can tell from the sound of her voice that she is literally floating, so euphoric is she about Yuga's existence.

Miu is way too young to start growing cynical about relationships.

She deserves to have, for once, this feeling of being so in love your feet don't quite touch the ground.

(10)

The Moon Stomp in Koenji is smaller than most American kitchens, and it really does have a kitchen, where sweet-smelling pizza and hot spicy curry are getting cooked up, but what's really cooking is the music.

Miu wanted me to come and hear her play with Yuga's band.

I'm trying not to expect too much, but I need not have worried.

Descend from the streets into that tiny smoke-filled club, packed with kids in hats and T-shirts, and the music there is so feel-good, giggles-provoking and harmonious Japanese-style it's like soaking in sudsy lukewarm tub water.

Admission is 2,500 yen for an all-you-can-eat meal-included evening of music.

Merrychan is a trio that performs original Japanese-language versions of Cuban and other Latin music.

Hearing Japanese sung and yelled in Latin fashion is somehow funnier than you'd think. Speak about identity crisis and parodying Japan's imitative modern music scene!

See how "Gerohaita! (He barfed!)" almost sounds Spanish? It's that wit in not taking oneself too seriously that makes these musicians rise above their otherwise proficient but pretty hunkydory (I mean, how could a bunch of Japanese kids beat Los Van Van?) musicianship to something unique, and something definitely entertaining.

No wonder the crowd (of about 30, half of them members of the other performing bands) is ecstatic.

Funyakotsu-ting was a geeky looking pudgy guy with glasses and a T-shirt with a picture of a donkey that says in English: "Bad Ass." He sang, narrated tales and even performed karaoke with a guitar.

A far cry from a demonstration of musical technique or artistic message, the almost-freak-show "otaku" performance still exuded a strange utterly disarming charm.

Several fans sat in the front row with multicolored light-sticks and swayed them in time to the music on one tune like they were at a Budokan rock concert.

More straight-ahead but just as hippie-spirited was Cigarette She Was, a folk/pop band starring guitar-strumming singer Teruyuki Kawabata. The groups were selling their CDs for something like 200 yen, the equivalent of $1.50.

Yuga plays kpanlogo in this band, his deep eyes _ those that Miu says look like those of an elephant _ buried in his long black hair as he plays with quiet concentration. He is sometimes so serious his upper lip seems to curl up in a haughty snarl.

Miu is so happy she can barely sit still as she jumps around, shaking a wooden stick covered with jangling bells.

I sit in one of the front seats surrounded by the cuddly noises and the warm smell of food and forget all thoughts.

It's a numbing feeling of thoughtless and humble satisfaction.

Who would have imagined that just a couple of months later Miu would break up with Yuga?

They are so young maybe it was to be expected.

She says it started with a quarrel about how to play a musical phrase in a rehearsal in their tiny apartment.

But when she shouted back, he slapped her then pushed her down on the tatami mat.

"I almost hit my head on the corner of his desk," Miu tells me, horrified.

She has to move out immediately, and so I have to go pick her up in our car.

Perhaps hoping to stop her from leaving, Yuga told her that he couldn't end the painful cycle of violence: He was beaten as a child while he was growing up.

His parents were very strict with him because he was an only child and they had such great hopes for him.

He was the kind of kid who couldn't even ask for a toy.

The parents would spank him and beat him and kick him and push him out, even in the winter, naked out into the backyard, although he screamed and stamped his little feet and cried as though his little lungs would tear into pieces.

But sometimes, when he feels that rage burn inside him, he is still that kid, and he can't stop himself when he wants to set things right and he must hit that person in front of him whom he loves so dearly yet who is acting in a way that he despises.

"It's totally messed up," Miu says. "He says he can't forgive his father, but I am not going to forgive him."

It is a sad end to a totally peaceful, hippie story of young love and brainlessly joyous music.

Or so I thought _ except that wasn't the end at all.

(11)

The details, when put together, make for a rather fascinating profile of a young man.

Maybe because I am a writer I am by nature intrigued by descriptions of things that people do that offer insight into human nature that writers see as a mission to explore.

I still don't really know Yuga at all.

I only know what Miu told me.

Maybe she is telling only her side of what happened as people are apt to do.

And maybe she didn't even really know him either.

The bits and pieces came slowly and gradually.

But as our conversation went on, the crimes, the shortcomings, the mistakes of Yuga came from her in torrents.

Yuga had another identity, Miu says.

He went to clubs to pick up women.

For this, he went by a false name, Ryuga, which still sounded enough like Yuga so that if someone called out the name _ someone who really knew who he was, who happened to be at the same club, the same party, or the same sidewalk, "Hey, Yuga!" _ the girl he was trying to seduce wouldn't find out he had told her his false name, the lie, the other identity: The boy who wasn't a poor musician at all but an up-and-coming recruit at a PR firm, who had money and was on his path to fame.

"That is so sad," Miu said to me, scoffing and sneering, although she was almost going to cry.

"I thought I came to Japan to find human relationships that were devoid of the separation of racism, to link with people in a way that wasn't tainted by the barriers of racial stereotypes. I just wanted a man who would look at me and not see a Jap before he saw anything else."

I touched her shoulder, pale and frail and trembling.

But nothing I could do or say was going to make Miu feel better.

When Yuga was Ryuga, when he wasn't practicing with Miu and the rest of his band, when he wasn't poring over his studies, he was talking to strange women as Ryuga in darkly deafening club after club, whispering strange nothings into their ears.

(12)

I'm sitting in a stuffy waiting room, not bothering to wonder why the others, troubled looking women of all ages and shapes, would need to be there.

It is clear birth is not the reason we are all here, even the nurses in pale pink outfits and the feminist gynecologist with the stern voice.

I am too nervous and worried to feel shame or guilt.

I just want Miu to come out from behind the curtains where she has gone—safe and alive and in one piece and the job done.

This is not a good feeling.

But this is all I can think.

We have all been there—our legs open—to remind us of what we did, not with just anyone but a man we truly loved but maybe who didn't love us enough—the chilly metal enters like an uncutting but unfeeling knife, merciless, guiltless, sinless until our drugged minds leave us—start counting: one, two, three, four—like angels who have given up.

And we feel nothing and we remember nothing.

We do not think of the baby that was, that could have been, that never was.

It is a tiny wormlike thing that must be removed like a bloody tumor because it is not a human being yet.

And I only want her to come out of there from behind the sterile curtains, safe and healthy and smiling.

I know she doesn't want to part with this human being that never was.

She wanted it to go on and on, feeling that person inside of her.

"It's not something to do immediately; that's not right," she says.

She has waited a week alone. She has not told anyone.

I don't realize this: All I am thinking about is her, not the thing that is inside of her.

But the baby who never was is that grandchild who never was, the future of the race, generations to come, who looks like your grandfather, your father, your son, the man you love, those little feet that run to you and bring snotty cheek against cheek, filled with life when you are only nearing death.

When she finally comes out of her drugged sleep, walks courageously to me in the waiting room, faking a smile, her breath smells like an old woman.

Love Poem

I like
The feel of your pulsating fibers
Beneath the golden muscles beneath my fingertips baby clams
Stuck against the window pane goldfish bowl
That run soft throbs along your veins blue-pink rivers
Jutting gently against your skin against my skin
While I rub rub rub
Your naked chest
In time and at times beats slower to our rhythms tingling
so good
So good feelings send me out to the ozone
Your hair
Black Black
Thick, straight, glistening in the light
Dark threads of seaweed bending
Asian hair
Hard stubbles lining your chin
Tickling
Playful pine needles matsu on my lips
Bounce on the roundness of my belly
Curved niches between the hip bones
Your eyes
Are my eyes
That see and see what I have seen;
They can't ever understand
The love of a Japanese woman
Who waits
Paled powdered hands
Eyes downcast night pools of wetness
Fifteen years for her samurai lover
And when he comes back

Nothing's changed
Nothing's changed

love hurts

love hurts
why does it hurt so much?
though i would rather suffer in love
than be without
it's so true
what they say:
that pain
hurting/squeezing/screaming
like a hole burrowing the insides of your heart
black and red
burning scars
i wish i could
forget/escape/disown
love
this love that makes us so brave
this love that makes us love so
much with that love
so the pain is
almost too much to bear
except in love:
to love not only those we
love
but love those whom
those we love
love
love hurts

love over time

if you have to ask
it is not love
you would be there
right now
making that love
over time
even
if it is not
love now
if you can think
it is not love
life without your
lover
giving that love
over time
grows
into love
forever

Transcending age, sex and race

When we get old, very very old, so old we are covered with wrinkles and our skin is pale and our breasts shrivel and droop and an old man looks and smells no different from an old woman, do we finally and once and for all transcend the barriers
of sex and race?
By succumbing to the all-unifying power of age and soon-to-come death, do we victoriously overcome the hurt of sex and the murder of race and the divisions we must inherit as legacy of mankind like the taint of original sin?
When we get up in the morning and look at what looks back at us in the mirror, will we no longer fear society's taunts for how we look and for the petty but definitive prisons of groupings for which we stand and must represent?
Will we at last have the choice of being nothing and so be someone who will not be defined by sex and race, and it will no longer matter whether you are man or woman, black, white or yellow?

The Father and The Son

My father is a lump of meat. He was not always this way.

He is still big. The beige sauce that hangs in a plastic bag above his bed pours into his intestines through a hole in the side of his bulging abdomen, feeding him effortlessly without the gorging, smacking of lips that used to be his favorite pastime.

My father used to work for NASA. I used to be asked what my father did for a living. People would wonder why a person so physically Japanese would speak perfect English with a Southern accent. NASA engineers worked in Huntsville, Alabama. I went to high school there while my father helped send people to the moon.

More than once, my colleagues at The Tokyo Times, Japan's largest English-language newspaper, where I now work, would ask me in their characteristically patronizing tone: "Do you know what 'a rocket scientist' refers to when someone uses the expression: 'You don't have to be a rocket scientist'?"

I never found rockets particularly glamorous. I used to detest them. I used to dread going to see rockets on display in Florida during vacation, or having to sit in family gatherings in living rooms watching NASA videos of launches.

The rocket scientist is now speechless.

He cannot breathe any more than he can swallow. A hole in his throat keeps him breathing, although a nurse periodically must probe the hole with a suction tube to drain out mucus so he won't suffocate on his own phlegm.

His big appetite and his big voice used to dominate our family dinner table.

I used to hate the sound of his chewing.

Sometimes, things would get dramatically worse, and I got beaten.

He'd reach out and smack me across the cheek. I would get thrown off my chair. I would see yellow stars circle in my head just like the Saturday morning cartoons. My cheek felt numb as though it had turned into rubber.

The causes for such outbursts have never been fully analyzed. I must have said the wrong thing, as young people tend to do, something too defiant, something too abrasive, something too honest.

Years later, after I got married, I had a chance to diplomatically ask my father why he was so angry back in those days.

He said he couldn't remember.

I guess sending people to the moon can get pretty stressful.

I was in first grade when I was called "Jap" for the first time.

A fat white boy taunted me from the street as I was looking out the window from my school bus.

"What's a Jap?" I asked my father.

I'd never forget the anger in his face.

"You must answer back," he said. "You must tell him, 'Yankee, go home!'"

It didn't make any sense. That's the slogan Japanese activists shouted against the U.S. Occupation. We weren't even in Japan anymore. We were in the Washington D.C. area then because my father was still working on his Ph.D.

I peer over the bed to look into his face. The stroke hasn't changed his chubby face, glowing with hardly a wrinkle.

He suddenly opens his eyes. They are slightly out of focus, comically cock-eyed, giving him a pathetic stunned, almost deranged, look.

A stench filters through the hole in his throat, and through his mouth he can't completely close, though he can't eat, breathe or speak.

"Otoosama," I say, using the honorific for "father."

He studies my face, slowly, like a digital camera waiting to focus its lens on a new unexpected object in its way.

His eyes open wider, sheer fear crossing over his crooked eyeballs.

Tears brim in my eyes.

"You don't have to be afraid," I tell him without speaking. "I am not going to hit you. I am not going to hit you."

I reach out and hold his hand, grasping his fingers in what ends up to be a power salute, although I'm not trying to give him the power salute.

His thumb moves erratically but with a force that's unmistakable.

His thumb touches my thumb, playfully swishing about, caressing the sides of the skin, dodging, pushing, in "yubi-zumo," a "finger-wrestling" game that kids played when Japan wasn't modern and we didn't have all those Made-in-Japan, now Made-in-China, gadget toys.

The thumb that can push the other's thumb down in a hold for a count of 10 wins.

I let him win.

Some people said the professor—my father worked as a professor in Japan after retiring from his stint at NASA—was now "a vegetable."

This is inaccurate because my father was not unconscious. Some people said he was "brain dead," but that was totally inaccurate.

He kept his eyes closed much of time, but in the beginning he would try to talk, opening and closing his mouth like a goldfish gasping for air.

He could only make gurgling noises in his chest, and no one could understand a thing he was trying to say.

My teen-age son, who adored his grandfather, would even mimic his noises and laugh.

In a matter of weeks, the rocket scientist turned professor gave up, and stopped trying to talk.

If he had been a real vegetable or brain dead, then that would have in a way simplified things, as he wouldn't have really been there—at least not in the way we remembered him.

He wasn't there in the way we remembered him, exactly, either. But he was still there.

That was the problem.

But such problems have a way of giving way to other more pressing problems, like deadlines at The Tokyo Times.

My editors were the typical washed out "gaijin" who had stayed in Japan too long, gotten used to the special Occupation-style treatment they were doled out in Japan, this land of geisha and hot-spring massages, that before they knew it found themselves frightened by the sheer idea of going back and being judged in a free-market competition-rules all-men-are-created-equal land-of-opportunity America.

Their job consisted mainly of sitting around in a circle in the office, sorting through wire service copy and pretending to edit, while worrying more about their more lucrative jobs teaching English and book deals with publishers eager to ride on the "Japan is cool" fad.

As a reporter, I was busy, not only writing articles but also watching my back from sinister attacks from these editors with fragile egos.

Every reporter learns the art of self-defense against editors fairly quickly. The 101 of journalism is to block it all out and focus on your own work.

Works of fiction are treated with respect. Editors ask your permission to change one word, to change a comma to a period.

Not so with articles.

Sometimes, you are lucky if you recognize anything that still speaks of yourself in the article after a stream of editors gets done with putting in their two cents worth, their fingerprint, their value, their proof of a higher paycheck than yours well earned.

You want to scream after seeing what these editors do to stories.

Reporters I work with say, with a straight face, they spend more energy figuring out how each editor edits than on reporting, and writing in that style to protect their stories from weird changes.

Sadly, at The Tokyo Times, a reporter has nowhere to turn for poetic justice.

Still, these problems are just jokes compared to real heartbreak.

Heartbreak is the universal human experience of feeling an important organ shatter into a zillion pieces inside of you.

It is excruciating pain.

Historically, this expression has been used to describe unrequited love or breaking up in romantic relationships.

But heartbreak is what I ended up feeling when my son became lovers with an older woman at a PR agency, the Tokyo branch of a global company.

It seemed the perfect job for him while on summer vacation from college. It paid relatively well because of his bilingual skills.

No one had bargained for that female executive in her 30s, "career woman," as the Japanese call it, a new statistic amid the social changes in this nation, where people, both male and female, are staying single longer, rejecting the traditional role models of bread-winner husband and stay-at-home housewife.

Yoko, executive vice president, should have been the paragon of feminist virtue. Instead, she was a prowler, pouncing on a teen-ager, a sexual harasser.

"Oh, Mom, she is so professional. She is so—so—together," he said purposely using a word from my generation to appease me.

"She knows all the Japanese ways of talking to clients, all those rules like how to win them over so they don't complain. She knows where everybody is supposed to sit according to the hierarchy at meetings, and all the proper phrasings and etiquette."

Age is not supposed to matter in love.

But I hated watching my son answer phone calls at 2 a.m. from Yoko, rush out of the house to see her. My son was also getting threatening calls from a Swede whom Yoko used to live with.

My son was not particularly worried about the Swede, although I was about to call the police, but he would call in a frenzied voice that I had to record a TV show he had promised to watch for Yoko, but had forgotten all about—some soap-operatic drama about a man's undying love for a woman dying of cancer.

He told me they had to sit around and have discussions about the show. He was in deep trouble if she found out he had missed an episode.

He also learned new names like Glenfiddich. He went on overnight business trips, playing mainly briefcase-carrier for Yoko.

I had an opportunity to meet Yoko at a hotel reception party for a major electronics company that her PR agency had a contract with and, it turned out, The Tokyo Times, wanted a story on.

She brought me a cup of tea. She held her own cup with both hands, demurely, a gracious thin smile constantly on her lips, and sipped on it without drinking.

"What are you thinking?" I asked abruptly in Japanese, not bothering with introductions and the obligatory business-card exchange. "He is just a kid. What do you think you are doing?"

She didn't blink. Her slant eyes stayed fixed on the tea cup. She had a bland Noh-mask face, except for flabby cheeks that made her face even more masklike. Perhaps this is Japanese beauty, I thought.

"I am extremely sorry for the concerns that this may have brought on you, Mother," she said.

I'm not your mother, I wanted to shout.

But I said: "What do you see in my son?"

"I realize you may see me as unworthy because of my age," she said, raising her tone half an octave in a characteristic yodeling throat trick of a Japanese "enka" singer. "I looked up, and your son was just there."

"Is this just a fling?" I asked, hoping it would be.

"I am not capable of flings," she said, giggling like a warbling geisha.

My son found my behavior unacceptable. He was moving out, he announced, to live with Yoko at her Roppongi apartment complex. He will finish college, he said, but he has made up his mind to marry Yoko.

I had tried to raise my son to be proud of his Japanese roots. But I was not prepared for this gaijin-inspired infatuation he was displaying of the stylized stereotypical Japanese woman.

Instead of the dollish "kawaii" girls in Shibuya, dressed like maids and clowns, in frills and polka-dots, he had picked the kimono-clad shuffling woman of the Edo Period, the one who knew how to walk three paces behind the samurai, the one well versed in the rules of the pecking order.

This was nothing other than self-hate—the manifestation of that perpetual mentality of racism that results in the rejection by the minority male of the minority female (or the minority female of the minority male) and enslaving worship of the majority race, so the ugliest member of the opposite sex of the majority race is by definition more attractive than the most beautiful member of the opposite sex of the minority race.

Except in this case, ironically, the race was the same—Asian.

My son was that ghetto boy, the American of Japanese ancestry, who was ashamed of how he wasn't a true proper Japanese—like Yoko so surely was.

"The value of an object is determined by the perceiver," my son wrote to me in a cell-phone e-mail after he moved out. "Is Yoko an old selfish hag? Or is she a beautiful Japanese woman?"

I felt my heart break inside of me. It crumbled. My chest pinched so tight as though every muscle there cramped tight like a fist, leaving just a giant hole there like the one in outer space where you drop endlessly forever and ever in your deepest dreams.

"I do not hate you," he wrote. "You are my mother and always will be."

This is heartbreak—when you can't love your own son.

Japanese funerals are rigid and proper like everything else Japanese. Maybe the rules are there so people can forget their sorrows. There are so many rules it's impossible to be sad for long.

These days, the funeral has become a modern business. Companies charge a lot of money, but all you have to do is pick out everything in a catalogue, including the altar set-ups at the funeral hall, gifts for the guests, the lunch menu.

The bald-headed Buddhist priest in embroidered robes chants for about half an hour in some ancient language that not even Japanese understand, banging on a bell or another percussion instrument, allegedly for effect, but I suspect to prevent us from dozing off.

The most dramatic moment is when the mourners toss flowers into the coffin before it heads out to the nearby cremation facility.

It is practically obligatory for Japanese to weep at this final farewell.

But I never feel sad at such moments because I can't turn my emotions off and on like a faucet.

If anything, I have a hard time not bursting out laughing at Japanese funerals.

Some of the dumbest things feel irresistibly funny. The words of the priest's chants sound like an obscenity in English. Someone stumbles accidentally while walking up to offer incense at the altar. A distant relative has to make an impeccably sorrowful face that's so obnoxiously pretentious and fake.

The van for carrying the coffin is a station wagon with a garish glittery gold and black-lacquer miniature temple on top of its roof.

Family members must pay the priest a lot of money to have a post-mortem name for the deceased believed to guarantee entry into the after-life.

I do not know my father's religious name offhand. These are long names with difficult characters, as befitting the tens of thousands of yen paid to get it, not simple Baptism and Confirmation names like Magdalene or Peter.

I did not look into the coffin as I tossed in a handful of white chrysanthemums.

It was sheer relief he had been released from that body.

I wanted to celebrate for my father.

But I kept quiet as we sat in a room, sipping tea and eating stale rice crackers, waiting for my father's body to get cooked in the giant oven at the cremation facility.

Japanese men get away with wearing a dark suit but women don't get off so easy.

Mourning clothes for women are sold in fancy department stores, the strangest dresses, based on Bette Davis movies probably, with no relevance to the realities of today, but worn always with a strand of pearls.

It's clear at first sight I am not properly dressed for this whole affair. I am wearing a black jacket and black pants, no pearls, my feeble attempt at mourning attire.

I have no time to contemplate this embarrassment as my son walks over and sits next to me.

He has broken up with Yoko, he tells me.

He neglected to tell me before, but every time he had tried to break up, she had threatened suicide. That was why he was running over there all the time at wee hours of the morning, he says.

Yoko was taken to the hospital for a failed suicide attempt and is now on medication.

"Dealing with Yoko is very unpleasant," he says. "You can't imagine what it's been like."

The clockwork's stopping comes slowly. Hot flashes are reminders of what's no longer going to work. No more menstrual cycles, no more reproduction. No more that egg traveling in that burning red womb inside of you, waiting for that lowly sperm to come, swimming like puny pathetic tadpoles up the river, fractions of the size, or glamour, of jumping salmon going to their deaths, sometimes that fertilization unwanted, miscarrying or aborted, red bleeding blood red, but that time when birth is planned, desired, a gift, like Baby Jesus, crying out in the wilderness in the sterile hospital bed, red blood on his face, my son, with tiny hands and feet, moving, and he looks into my eyes, so wise, so perfect, and we have known each other for all eternity, red, those hot flashes tell you about that heat, burning, that place inside that never forgets.

Menopause sex is an affirmation of this legacy.

That is why it is human duty to perform this act regularly, like a religious ritual, in homage, in honor, to give thanks, no matter its futility in reproductory functionality.

My husband's arms still feel muscular and strong in the dark. His tongue and fingers against my breast and nipple feel warm, ticklish, as though the cells on my body are hyperactive, peeking from everywhere, waiting to rub against his cells, his prickly face, his biceps, his stomach against my stomach, his hardened penis. The skin is supposed to sag, wrinkle and shrivel with age, but everything instead feels taut and tight, so persistent and frantic, and we are young again, no, ageless, two people caught in time, waiting to die and be reborn and meet again, to have our son again, as the hot flashes explode in my abdomen in orgasm, popping red colors in my brain.

Someday, I'm going to build a house, my son once said when he was a toddler.

It's going to have music, books, and lots and lots of flowers, he said in that tiny voice children have that's so disarming and endearing like a kitten's meow.

Years later when he was in high school, my son told me a white schoolmate had laughed at him for wearing a Jimi Hendrix

T-shirt. You don't even know who that is, you foreigner, the child had said.

"I grew up on Jimi Hendrix. My dad plays Jimi Hendrix solos, note for note," my son, the only Asian in his class, had said.

There is an old photo of my son, playing a toy guitar, standing knee-high next to my husband with his Fender. The boy has a strained look on his face, as though he is really sending that guitar wailing.

I see he has that same look on stage.

At a shabby cramped basement club in Koenji, where the smell of curry wafts everywhere, mixing with the beat of funky traps drumming, my son is playing blues guitar with other "freeter" Japanese youngsters in a band called Cigarette Box.

It was difficult finding the place, even with directions printed off the Internet. Except for a tiny sign, there is no clue above ground that this club exists like so many others scattered across Tokyo.

The crowd here appears to be mostly members of other bands waiting to play. They clap enthusiastically after every song as though they have been victims as misfit freaks of "ijime" bullying from more decent conformist Japanese while growing up and don't want to hurt anybody's feelings, if they can help it.

Huge warped pots of curry and rice sit on the counter, next to platefuls of fragrant pizza. It's all you can eat for a few hundred yen, complete with free drinks. I ask for tomato juice, and the boy behind the counter gives me a huge glass with ice cubes and a big straw.

They don't look around nervously as most Japanese do in crowds. Some are wearing funny hats. Their jeans are raggedy and have holes. They would fit right in, in Berkeley.

They sing about gratitude for compassion, memories of blowing bubbles in the air, their pet cat, rainbow clouds and flowers, hangovers, and lost love.

They squirm on stage, jump around, scream, banter with the crowd. People chuckle and shout back answers.

My son's new girlfriend Miu is the violinist for Cigarette Box.

She works at a record store in Akihabara but also plays with techno artists and a "world music" band.

She slaps me on the back when she sees me, in between sets.

My son doesn't like talking about this, but they met on the Internet. There are networking sites that help Japanese musicians find people to play with.

I found this out, rather accidentally from Miu, when we had lunch together at a pasta place in Shibuya on a weekend.

She said she took along the male harmonium player from her world music band, just in case, to the first jam session with my son. She figured meeting someone on the Net could be dangerous.

"But it was like I got sucked in, watching him play," she said as though mesmerized. "I couldn't play anything."

I bought a hat for Miu at the Shibuya 109 shopping complex because she looks good in hats.

She also looks good in mini-skirts, torn jeans, fake fur, dangling earrings, just about anything. She has a red blister on her neck from practicing her violin.

I hate to say this. After Yoko, anybody halfway normal was okay by me. But Miu is too good to be true. When she plays, I love her so much I feel like crying.

Bring out the violins—for real.

I am afraid, I tell Miu. I am getting old. My father is dead. As time passes, I will get older and older.

I don't know why I am telling her this.

She has barely been around on this planet for some 20 years, and she doesn't know a thing about getting old.

I don't know if I did the right thing.

My son is trying to play music instead of seeking a steady job at a PR firm. He is no more Jimi Hendrix than his father is, or ever will be, and I can't really help him because I am just a reporter.

We are mere insignificant dots on the cosmic map, even more difficult to find than this club was in the night backstreets of Tokyo. The only reason I am not too afraid now is because the music is so loud I can't think straight.

Things will work out. You will enter a new stage in life, Miu says.

There's a strange finality that's somehow reassuring.

Miu looks at me and then whispers into my ear: "The most important thing to know is that everything is going to be okay."

Acknowledgments

Some of the works in this collection previously appeared in the following publications, and acknowledgement is gratefully made to their editors. They include the author's first poetry collection: *Peeling* (I. Reed Books, 1988); the anthologies: *POW WOW: Charting the Fault Lines in the American Experience—Short Fiction from Then to Now* (Da Capo Press, 2009), *On a Bed of Rice*, (Anchor Books, 1995), *The Stories We Hold Secret: Tales of Women's Spiritual Development* (Greenfield Review Press, 1986), and *Breaking Silence: An Anthology of Contemporary Asian American Poets* (Greenfield Review Press, 1983); the broadside package, *Beyond Rice*; the literary journals: *Obras, San Francisco Stories, Mango, Konch, Y'Bird, Echoes From Gold Mountain, Ally, Asian Journal, Bridge, Coydog Review, The Greenfield Review, Hokubei Mainichi, Kyoto Review, Oro Madre, River Styx, Soup, Suisun Valley Review, Women Talking, Women Listening, Yellow Silk*, and *Zone*, as well as *The Oakland Tribune* newspaper.

Some works have also been performed or read at the Bowery Poetry Club in New York City; the San Francisco Museum of Modern Art, the Asian American Theater Workshop, the Chinese Cultural Center and the Nihonmachi Streetfair in San Francisco; the Kuraki Noh Theater in Yokohama; and Shinobazu no Ike at Ueno Park, the Pink Cow, Bunga, What the Dickens, Ben's Café, "Paint Your Teeth," and other art spots and events in Tokyo.

About the Author

Yuri Kageyama is a poet, writer and journalist of bilingual and bicultural upbringing, who was born in Japan and grew up in Maryland, Tokyo and Alabama. Her first book, *Peeling*, a collection of poems, was published by I. Reed Press in 1988.

Her works in English have also appeared in many literary publications, including *Y'Bird*, *Greenfield Review*, *Obras*, *Beyond Rice*, *River Styx*, *San Francisco Stories*, *Yellow Silk*, and *Konch* and the anthologies: *Breaking Silence: an Anthology of Asian American Poets* (Greenfield Review Press, 1983); *POW WOW: Charting the Fault Lines in the American Experience—Short Fiction from Then to Now* (Da Capo Press, 2009); *MultiAmerica: Essays on Cultural Wars and Cultural Peace* (Viking, Penguin, 1997), *On a Bed of Rice* (Anchor Books, 1995), *The Stories We Hold Secret: Tales of Women's Spiritual Development* (Greenfield Review Press, 1986) and *Other Side River: Contemporary Japanese Women's Poetry* (Stone Bridge Press, 1995). Her poetry, translated into Japanese, is featured in a 1985 anthology of Japanese-American and Japanese-Canadian poetry published by Doyo Bijutsusha and a 1993 book co-written with Hamao Yokota, on the Japanese workplace, was published in Japanese. Her column on motherhood, called "Oya Baka Notes," appeared in San Francisco's Japanese-American newspaper *Hokubei Mainichi*.

Talking TAIKO (March 2010), directed by Yoshiaki Tago, documents Yuri Kageyama's readings and thoughts on writing, art and life on film.

She has read with Ishmael Reed, Shuntaro Tanikawa, Eric Kamau Gravatt, Geraldine Kudaka, Victor Hernandez Cruz,

Winchester Nii Tete, Russel Baba, Seamus Heaney, Yumi Miyagishima, Shozu Ben, Keiji Kubo, Teruyuki and Haruna Kawabata, Abel Coelho, Yuri Matsueda and many others. Her collaborations, involving music, visual arts and dance, include a performance at an Isamu Noguchi exhibit at the San Francisco Museum of Modern Art. Most recently, as Yuricane, she performs her writing in collaboration with musicians Toshinori Takimoto and Takenari Shibata.

A Back Alley Asian American Love Story, of Sorts, a film directed by Niccolo Caldararo of Kageyama's short story, was shown at the San Francisco and New York Asian American film festivals, and won awards at the 1986 Palo Alto Film Festival, 1987 Ann Arbor Film Festival and 1988 Onion City Film Festival.

Yuri Kageyama appears in David Mura's memoir *Turning Japanese*, which also features excerpts of her work. She is compiling, with Isao Tokuhashi, an oral history of composer and master taiko-drummer Yoichi Watanabe, leader of Amanojaku, a Tokyo taiko group where her son Isaku Kageyama is a drummer, besides leading the taiko-rock group Hybrid Soul.

Yuri Kageyama is a magna cum laude graduate of Cornell University and holds an M.A. in Sociology from the University of California, Berkeley. She lives in Tokyo.